New Directions for
Higher Education

Betsy O. Barefoot
Jillian L. Kinzie
CO-EDITORS

Exploring Diversity at Historically Black Colleges and Universities: Implications for Policy and Practice

Robert T. Palmer
C. Rob Shorette II
Marybeth Gasman
EDITORS

Number 170 • Summer 2015
Jossey-Bass
San Francisco

EXPLORING DIVERSITY AT HISTORICALLY BLACK COLLEGES AND UNIVERSITIES:
IMPLICATIONS FOR POLICY AND PRACTICE
Robert T. Palmer, C. Rob Shorette II, Marybeth Gasman
New Directions for Higher Education, no. 170
Betsy O. Barefoot and Jillian L. Kinzie, Co-editors

Microfilm copies of issues and articles are available in 16mm and 35mm, as well as microfiche in 105mm, through University Microfilms Inc., 300 North Zeeb Road, Ann Arbor, MI 48106-1346.

NEW DIRECTIONS FOR HIGHER EDUCATION (ISSN 0271-0560, electronic ISSN 1536-0741) is part of The Jossey-Bass Higher and Adult Education Series and is published quarterly by Wiley Subscription Services, Inc., A Wiley Company, at Jossey-Bass, One Montgomery Street, Suite 1200, San Francisco, CA 94104-4594. Periodicals Postage Paid at San Francisco, California, and at additional mailing offices. POSTMASTER: Send address changes to New Directions for Higher Education, Jossey-Bass, One Montgomery Street, Suite 1200, San Francisco, CA 94104-4594.

New Directions for Higher Education is indexed in Current Index to Journals in Education (ERIC); Higher Education Abstracts.

Individual subscription rate (in USD): $89 per year US/Can/Mex, $113 rest of world; institutional subscription rate: $335 US, $375 Can/Mex, $409 rest of world. Single copy rate: $29. Electronic only–all regions: $89 individual, $335 institutional; Print & Electronic–US: $98 individual, $402 institutional; Print & Electronic–Canada/Mexico: $98 individual, $442 institutional; Print & Electronic–Rest of World: $122 individual, $476 institutional.

Editorial correspondence should be sent to the Co-editor, Betsy O. Barefoot, Gardner Institute, Box 72, Brevard, NC 28712.

Cover design: Wiley
Cover Images: © Lava 4 images | Shutterstock

www.josseybass.com

CONTENTS

Editors' Notes

A report from the Center for Minority Serving Institutions at the University of Pennsylvania has underscored the changing racial demography of historically Black colleges and universities (HBCUs) (Gasman, 2013). Specifically, this report has shown that the population currently enrolled in HBCUs is made up of roughly 76% Black students, with the remainder composed of other racial and ethnic groups. Indeed, the racial demography of HBCUs looks completely different today from in the 1950s when the student body of HBCUs was nearly 100% Black. Despite the increase in the enrollment of non-Black students at HBCUs, limited research has examined the experiences of racially and ethnically diverse students as well as other underrepresented students at these institutions.

Interestingly, while research has shown that HBCUs have always welcomed racially and ethnically diverse populations (Foster, Miller, & Guyden, 1999), research has noted that some stakeholders at HBCUs feel that the increasing diversity, both racial and otherwise, of Black colleges could radically change their institutional culture, climate, and mission, thereby threatening the historical mission and environment of these institutions. In fact, some feel that the preservation of the traditional climate of HBCUs is critical because it has been a salient facilitator of Black student success (Gasman, Baez, Drezner, Sedgwick, & Tudico, 2007).

Currently, more Black students are opting to attend predominantly White institutions and for-profit institutions than in years past (Patton, 2012). That fact, coupled with the impact of court cases (e.g., *Adams v. Richardson*, 1972, and *United States v. Fordice*, 1992), has compelled public HBCUs to increase the racial diversity of their campuses. Therefore, the number of non-Black students enrolling in HBCUs may continue to increase (Gasman et al., 2007). To respond to this likelihood, it is critical that the higher education community in general and HBCU leaders—administrators and key stakeholders specifically—engage in meaningful discourse about how these institutions can more intentionally embrace the changing demography on their campuses, especially in light of the concerns posed by some stakeholders. It is important to note that while this volume places particular attention on discussing the changing racial demography of HBCUs, it also discusses and provides critical context on other minority populations. Indeed, the volume seeks to examine the complexities of this issue

NEW DIRECTIONS FOR HIGHER EDUCATION, no. 170, Summer 2015 © 2015 Wiley Periodicals, Inc.
Published online in Wiley Online Library (wileyonlinelibrary.com) • DOI: 10.1002/he.20127

and offer recommendations for practice, policy, and future research to help HBCU leaders engage this critical issue.

In the first chapter, Marybeth Gasman and Thai-Huy Nguyen provide the foundation for this volume by providing some historical and contemporary context about diversity at HBCUs. In doing this, they challenge five myths related to diversity at HBCUs. These myths range from the racial makeup of the faculty at HBCUs to the perception that HBCUs are not able to help advance the nation's higher education goals. In Chapter 2, John Michael Lee Jr. calls attention to the institutional diversity of HBCUs. Moreover, while he also provides insight into these institutions' racial diversification, he argues that HBCUs must look beyond race and ethnicity to consider other forms of diversity, such as socioeconomic status, sexual orientation, and international status. In Chapter 3, Derek F. Greenfield, Tony Innouvong, Richard Jay Aglugub, and Ismail A. Yusuf reflect on their experiences as diverse students and professionals at an HBCU and discuss how these experiences impacted their racial and cultural identity development.

In Chapter 4, C. Rob Shorette II and Andrew T. Arroyo use national data to draw a picture of White students enrolled at 4-year HBCUs. In this chapter, they argue that despite the media's emphasis on an increase in the enrollment of White students at HBCUs, data show that a disproportionate number of White students are enrolling at 2-year, rather than 4-year, HBCUs. In Chapter 5, Robert T. Palmer, Dina C. Maramba, Taryn Ozuna Allen, and Ramon B. Goings provide an overview of factors that encourage Latino/a students to attend an HBCU, and they discuss the experiences of those students at a Black college. In Chapter 6, Steve D. Mobley Jr. and Jennifer M. Johnson draw from the extant literature on HBCUs to discuss some of the challenges that lesbian, gay, bisexual, and transgender (LGBT) students encounter at these institutions. They also provide a set of best practices to help HBCUs create a more affirming and inclusive campus climate for LGBT students.

In Chapter 7 of this volume, Valerie C. Lundy-Wagner provides an overview of how discussions of diversity have been treated in the existing literature on HBCUs. She also delineates how embracing a more expansive definition of diversity, beyond a Black-White paradigm, could provide HBCUs with leverage to become more engaged in the postsecondary policy arena. C. Rob Shorette II offers final thoughts to differentiate the contributions of this volume from other literature that focuses on HBCUs. He suggests a number of potential lines of future scholarly inquiry that would expand and enrich the knowledge base on diversity and HBCUs.

Not only does this volume of *New Directions for Higher Education* address the complexities of the changing demography of HBCUs, but it also identifies opportunities for HBCUs to create a more inclusive environment for all students who seek to enroll at these important institutions of higher education. Finally, this volume discusses ways in which HBCUs could use the changing landscape, racial and otherwise, as an opportunity for future growth and development. Indeed, given the range and the depth of the issues covered in this volume, we recommend it as a must read for anyone interested in HBCUs in general and student success within these institutions specifically.

Robert T. Palmer
C. Rob Shorette II
Marybeth Gasman
Editors

References

Adams v. Richardson, 351 f.2d. 636 (D.C. Cir. 1972).

Foster, L., Miller, A. L., & Guyden, J. A. (1999). Faculty diversity at historically Black colleges and universities: Context, scope, and meaning. In L. Foster, J. A. Guyden, & A. L. Miller (Eds.), *Affirmed action: Essays on the academic and social lives of White faculty members at historically Black colleges and universities* (pp. 183–191). Lanham, MD: Rowman & Littlefield.

Gasman, M. (2013). *The changing face of historically Black colleges and universities*. Philadelphia, PA: Center for Minority Serving Institutions, University of Pennsylvania.

Gasman, M., Baez, B., Drezner, N., Sedgwick, K., & Tudico, C. (2007). Historically Black colleges and universities: Recent trends. *Academe*, *93*(1), 69–78.

Patton, S. (2012, October 29). From cellblock to campus, one Black man defies the data. *The Chronicle of Higher Education*. Retrieved from http://chronicle.com/article /In-Terms-of-Gender/135294/

United States v. Fordice, 112 S. Ct. 2727 (1992).

ROBERT T. PALMER *is an associate professor of student affairs in the College of Community and Public Affairs at the State University of New York, Binghamton.*

C. ROB SHORETTE II *recently earned a PhD in higher education from Michigan State University. Dr. Shorette is an educator and researcher focused on diversity and equity in higher education, a former HBCU presidential aide, and an HBCU alumnus.*

MARYBETH GASMAN *is a professor of higher education in the Graduate School of Education at the University of Pennsylvania.*

NEW DIRECTIONS FOR HIGHER EDUCATION • DOI: 10.1002/he

1

This chapter provides a historical and contemporary overview of diversity at HBCUs, challenges five myths related to diversity at HBCUs, and concludes with opportunities for future research consideration on diversity at HBCUs.

Myths Dispelled: A Historical Account of Diversity and Inclusion at HBCUs

Marybeth Gasman, Thai-Huy Nguyen

In this chapter, we provide both a historical and a contemporary backdrop on diversity at historically Black colleges and universities (HBCUs). In particular, we provide evidence to dispel these five pervasive myths related to diversity and HBCUs:

1. HBCUs serve only Black students.
2. HBCUs have only Black faculty.
3. HBCUs do not have lesbian, gay, bisexual, and transgender (LGBT) students or centers.
4. HBCUs have only Christian students.
5. HBCUs are unable to advance our nation's higher education goals.

We then present unanswered questions and opportunities for new research in the area of diversity that we hope future scholars will tackle.

Myth 1: HBCUs Serve Only Black Students

Because HBCUs are "historically Black," many people assume that these institutions have served only Black students throughout their history and continue to serve only Black students today. However, at many HBCUs throughout the nation the first students were White. Often, the founders of HBCUs were Whites who had served in the Northern army and worked with the federal government's Freedmen's Bureau. In other situations, these White founders were missionaries who went south after the Civil War to educate the formerly enslaved Black population. Because they were serving in leadership roles at many of the American Missionary Association's Black colleges, Whites also sent their children to these institutions. In particular, at Howard University, founded in 1867, General Oliver O. Howard, the president, sent his daughters to the institution along with the daughters of another founder of Howard, making five White females the first students at Howard University. The presence of White females (or males for that matter) at HBCUs often was unreported because intermixing of the races during the period of the founding of HBCUs was highly taboo (Gasman, Lundy-Wagner, Ransom, & Bowman, 2010).

Although the majority of students at HBCUs during the institutions' formative years were Black, these colleges and universities were also home to international students from Europe and China. HBCU presidents often wanted to expose their students to new ideas and people from different cultures, and hosting international exchange students was one way to do this. At Fisk University in Nashville, Tennessee, President Charles Spurgeon Johnson knew that in order to take his students to a new level and expose them to outside forces beyond the South, entertaining exchange students on campus was necessary. Fisk had exchange programs with French, English, and Spanish colleges and universities as well as those in the Caribbean (Gilpin & Gasman, 2003). Of note, many of the international students visiting the Fisk campus would work hand in hand with Fisk students to fight and challenge American racism, attempting to integrate movie theaters and pushing back against "colored" and "White" drinking fountains. These students served as an inspiration for each other and an impetus for civil rights agitation (Gasman, 2001).

After de jure segregation ended in 1954, but before there was large-scale integration of colleges and universities, the United Negro College Fund, trying to establish a purpose for HBCUs in a post–legally segregated United States, surveyed White students in Northern states to see if they might be interested in attending HBCUs. Although Black college presidents were not deeply committed to enrolling large numbers of White students, they saw the writing on the wall after *Brown v. Board of Education* and knew that their institutions would be seen as vestiges of segregation—a label that would not be placed on the formerly all-White institutions. The survey showed that only a handful of White students were interested in attending HBCUs, as they considered HBCUs foreign in nature and assumed they were inferior institutions (Gasman, 2007). The integration of colleges and universities was certainly a gradual process, but by 1980, according to the National Center for Education Statistics (2011), White students made up 10% or more (up to 88%) of the student populations at 22% of all HBCUs (see Table 1.1).

Although *Brown v. Board of Education* enforced a federal mandate for institutions to integrate, the changes in racial composition at HBCUs were also affected by the growth in the Hispanic and Asian populations. The conversation pertaining to equal access to postsecondary education was no longer just a Black and White issue. For instance, Table 1.1 provides a list of HBCUs with student populations of 10% or more White students for the years 1980 and 2011. Institutions with less than 10% White students were

Table 1.1. Enrollment at Historically Black Colleges and Universities, 1980–2011

Institution	1980		2011		(2011–1980)	
	White	Black	White	Black	White	Black
North Carolina Central University	10%	88%	11%	77%	1%	−11%
University of the Virgin Islands	11%	71%	–	–	–	–
Central State University	11%	84%	–	–	–	–
Alabama A&M University	12%	66%	–	–	–	–
Elizabeth City State University	13%	86%	14%	72%	1%	−14%
Winston-Salem State University	13%	86%	17%	72%	4%	−14%
University of Arkansas at Pine Bluff	14%	84%	–	–	–	–
Fayetteville State University	15%	83%	17%	66%	2%	−17%
Langston University	16%	65%	14%	82%	−2%	17%
Harris-Stowe State University	17%	81%	–	–	–	–
Savannah State University	18%	75%	–	–	–	–
University of Maryland Eastern Shore	20%	74%	15%	69%	−5%	−5%
Bishop State Community College	21%	76%	30%	63%	9%	−13%
Tennessee State University	31%	63%	23%	70%	−8%	7%
Bowie State University	32%	62%	–	–	–	–
Delaware State University	35%	63%	14%	70%	−21%	7%
St. Philip's College	35%	24%	30%	11%	−5%	−13%
Lincoln University	50%	40%	58%	35%	8%	−5%
Kentucky State University	50%	48%	23%	53%	−27%	5%
Shelton State Community College	77%	23%	54%	34%	−23%	11%
West Virginia State University	81%	17%	56%	11%	−25%	−6%
Gadsden State Community College	82%	13%	69%	20%	−13%	7%
Bluefield State College	88%	10%	85%	10%	−3%	0%
J. F. Drake State Technical College	–	–	42%	51%	–	–
H. Councill Trenholm State Technical College	–	–	36%	61%	–	–
Lawson State Community College–Birmingham Campus	–	–	14%	75%	–	–

Source: U.S. Department of Education, National Center for Education Statistics, Integrated Postsecondary Education Data System (IPEDS), Fall 1980 and Fall 2011 Enrollment at Historically Black Colleges and Universities.

not included on this list. At first glance, one can see that not every HBCU with 10% or more White students in 1980 was on the list in 2011, and that three additional HBCUs—J. F. Drake State Technical College, H. Councill Trenholm State Technical College, and Lawson State Community College–Birmingham Campus—had at least a 4% to 32% increase in White students. Of the HBCUs that maintained at least a 10% White student enrollment in 2011, several institutions encountered steep reductions in that population. However, and most notably, seven HBCUs in 2011 also experienced a reduction in Black enrollment. St. Philip's College, for example, experienced a 5% reduction in White enrollment, as well as a 13% reduction in Black enrollment. Why is this the case? According to the U.S. Census Bureau (2011),

"More than half of the growth in the total population of the United States between 2000 and 2010 was due to the increase in the Hispanic population" (p. 3), and "the Asian population grew faster than any other major race group between 2000 and 2010" (p. 4). Our nation is rapidly changing, and the demand for postsecondary education is stronger than it has ever been, suggesting that U.S. postsecondary institutions must continue to widen their doors to different demographic groups in order to keep pace with the changing populace.

Today, 24% of students at HBCUs identify as non-Black, a striking difference from 1950 when these institutions were nearly 100% Black (Gasman, 2013). In the inaugural report, *The Changing Face of Historically Black Colleges and Universities*, released by the University of Pennsylvania's Center for Minority Serving Institutions, Gasman (2013) reports that much of the non-Black student population growth can be accounted for by multiple regions and states that have experienced significant changes in racial composition. As a case in point, one can look to the state of Texas. Prairie View A&M University has witnessed at 123% increase in Hispanic students between 1980 and 2011, while Texas College and Huston-Tillotson University have encountered a 9% and 19% proportional growth in Hispanic enrollment, respectively. Moreover, the top three HBCUs with the highest Asian-American enrollment are also in the Lone Star State. To insist that HBCUs serve *only* Black students is to ignore their historical mission and their growing potential to provide education to all, especially those who have been excluded by institutions that are unaware of or insensitive to the challenges brought on by limited opportunities and resources.

Myth 2: HBCUs Have Only Black Faculty

Much like general perceptions of HBCU students throughout these institutions' histories, the common belief about HBCU faculty is that they are also monolithic, representing only Blacks. Not only is this myth completely false, but also at all but a few HBCUs, the faculty was almost entirely White during the 1800s and early 1900s. The exceptions are the African Methodist Episcopal (AME) Church–related colleges, which were run by and staffed by free Blacks from the North who were active missionaries in the AME Church. However, all other HBCUs relied upon teachers from the North initially, and most of these teachers were White missionaries who had ventured south to address educational needs and bring their form of Christianity to Blacks.

Most HBCUs, again with the exception of the AME schools, did not have Black presidents until the mid-1930s or 1940s. Once these Black presidents, all male with the exception of Mary McLeod Bethune (Bethune Cookman College) and Willa Player (Bennett College), assumed leadership at these institutions, they began to hire additional Black faculty members.

Eventually, the faculties of HBCUs became predominantly Black, offering African-American scholars a place to teach, do research, and thrive (Thompson, 1973). Rarely were these scholars afforded similar opportunities at predominantly White institutions even when they were equally qualified and had earned their doctorates at mainstream research institutions (Anderson, 1997). Despite growing numbers of Black faculty members— the result of more and more African Americans attending college and choosing teaching as a profession—HBCUs remained open to White faculty.

During the 1940s and 1950s, in particular, Jewish faculty members at northern, predominantly White schools were often fired because of real and alleged ties to communism. HBCUs became safe havens for these individuals. Having been ostracized and after surviving their own Holocaust in the United States, African Americans could empathize with Jews and the discrimination that they felt. When these highly qualified Jewish professors needed a place to teach, HBCUs welcomed them with open arms, capitalizing on their academic talent in various fields, especially math and science (Edgcomb, 1993).

Although most Jewish professors found refuge at HBCUs, there were some who faced difficult situations on campus and had to move on or were fired. One such incident took place at Fisk University under the leadership of Charles Johnson. Lee Lorch, a prominent Jewish mathematician, was a popular faculty member on the Fisk campus. However, in 1954, he decided to enroll his White daughter in a Black Nashville public school to test the limits of the new law put forth by *Brown v. Board of Education*. Because of Lorch's action, in addition to accusations that he was a communist, the campus was under extreme pressure from funders to get rid of him. Johnson, as Fisk president, succumbed to the pressure and fired Lorch. Philander Smith College in Little Rock, Arkansas, then hired Lorch, but soon fired him as well, unable to withstand the controversy or to risk loss of White funding (Gasman, 1999). When HBCU presidents felt pressured and feared losing their sources of funding because of comments made by outspoken faculty, they chose the course of action they believed to be in the best interest of their institution over a particular faculty member's livelihood.

During the 1970s and 1980s, some White and Asian faculty members came to HBCUs, mainly to teach in the sciences as there was a dearth of Black faculty in this academic area. Once these individuals spread the word that teaching within the HBCU setting was acceptable, others came. Slowly, the numbers increased, and today only 57% of tenured and 64% of tenure-track faculty at HBCUs are Black (Gasman, 2013).

Certainly many Black faculty choose to teach at an HBCU because it represents a service to their communities and an opportunity to help pave the way for a new generation of students. Although the culture of HBCUs has been based on maintaining the conditions to support the achievement of their students, such as the hiring of diverse faculties, more recently

HBCUs have experienced a "brain drain," whereby the competition with majority institutions for Black faculty has been exceptionally fierce (Seymore, 2006). In effect, this has opened up several academic appointments for recent Black graduates. Moreover, a national study of minority-serving institutions (Conrad & Gasman, 2015) that included three HBCUs demonstrated that there is a push to broaden the hiring search—to recruit faculty from all walks of life—in order to expose their students to more different and competing beliefs and ideologies. Such a push to diversify the faculty is a reflection of some HBCUs' awareness of a new world that rewards students who possess the ability to work and collaborate with those different from themselves with greater opportunities.

Myth 3: HBCUs Do Not Have LGBT Students or Centers

Because of their historical mission, many HBCUs are challenged by a culture of social conservatism. They are unwilling to dismantle tradition for the sake of addressing an increasingly diverse and active generation of students who may identify as lesbian, gay, bisexual, or transgender (LGBT) or may deviate from social mores, such as by dressing in drag (Harper & Gasman, 2008). This conservatism has emerged from segments of Black communities (Cohen, 1999) such as the Black Protestant churches. Both churches and HBCUs continue to stigmatize their LGBT populations and create subcultures of fear, denial, and secrecy. This environment, which nurtures racial pride, creates conflict for LGBT-identifying students, especially as they progress through college and come to new realizations about themselves beyond their racial identity. Due to the historical relationship between HBCUs and the church, HBCUs have been slow in institutionalizing support for LGBT students by having a special resource center or faculty and staff training (Patton, 2011).

Despite these challenges, LGBT student populations certainly exist at HBCUs. The real question—the more pressing matter—is whether any LGBT students are open about their sexuality and comfortable about self-identifying to another person. The needs of these students, whether they are in or out of the closet, have significant implications for college student services (Nguyen, Samayoa, Mobley, & Gasman, 2014). There is no doubt that the LGBT population experiences prejudicial treatment by society, resulting in observed depression and negative behavior, such as unprotected sex and drug and alcohol abuse that lead to poor physical and psychological health outcomes (Brown, Danovsky, Lourie, DiClemente, & Ponton, 1997; Institute of Medicine, 2011). Studies suggest (Harper & Gasman, 2008; Nguyen et al., 2014; Patton, 2011) that the conditions in which students learn—listen, question, and engage in deep and meaningful conversations with faculty, staff, and other students—as well as the conditions that encourage them to socialize, interact, and develop and maintain open and honest relationships with others must be altered to signal to LGBT students that their presence is not merely tolerated, but truly valued.

In the past decade, HBCUs have been moving toward institutionalizing LGBT support services and establishing special centers to meet the needs of LGBT students. To date, 20% of HBCUs have an institutionalized center devoted to their LGBT communities (Gasman, 2013). LGBT support has come through specially trained student services personnel, centers, courses, and national conferences that spur conversation. For example, Howard University has had an on-campus support organization for gay and lesbian students since 2000. Bowie State University opened its Lesbian, Gay, Bisexual, Transgender, Queer, Intersex, and Allies Resource Center in 2012. Moreover, Morehouse College is offering its first LGBT course in 2013. The course will focus on Black gay, lesbian, bisexual, and transgender history and will be taught by a Yale faculty member via Skype. And Spelman College has been an exemplar among HBCUs, sponsoring a national conference in 2011 on HBCUs and LGBT issues. A small minority of HBCUs is leading the charge in addressing the challenges and supporting the needs of LGBT students.

Myth 4: HBCUs Have Only Christian Students

Religion is significant to both the historical foundation of HBCUs as well as the individual experiences of male and female Black students. While there is great variety among HBCUs in mission and environment today (Brown & Freeman, 2004), the majority of HBCUs were founded by religious missionaries, including members of the Baptist, Congregational, African Methodist Episcopal (AME), and African Methodist Episcopal Zion denominations (Gasman & Tudico, 2008; Williams & Ashley, 2004). These are all Christian denominations, and, as such, most HBCUs operate with a Christian ethos even when they are public and state-affiliated.

Although there is little discussion of religious differences among African Americans on HBCU campuses, there is great diversity among the student bodies. Students represent myriad religions from Muslim to Catholic to Protestant. Institutions such as Dillard University and Xavier University of Louisiana have large percentages of Catholic students due to their presence in New Orleans, where the Catholic Church is dominant. Institutions in more urban areas, including Spelman College, Morehouse College, Clark Atlanta University, and Morgan State University, have significant numbers of Muslim students (Gasman & Tudico, 2008). The existence of religious diversity, however, does not necessarily lead a campus to embrace different religious communities.

Beliefs and behaviors counter to the dominant religion on campus can result in divisive tension among factions of the community (Harper & Gasman, 2008; Nguyen et al., 2014). However, it is important to note that the campus climates of religiously affiliated HBCUs or those with a strong religious culture are no more likely to be strongly affected by religion than non-HBCUs with similar institutional structures and missions. In other words, HBCUs should not be singled out for their religious identity, nor should religion be utilized to develop a narrow understanding of their student bodies. If this rationale were to be used to make sense of HBCU student populations, then other institutions with a Christian history such as the College of William and Mary (public) or Harvard University (private) would also be thought to enroll "only Christian students" (Karabel, 2006). We know this is not true.

Myth 5: HBCUs Are Unable to Advance Our Nation's Higher Education Goals

In 1866, HBCUs educated Black students from every background, and even as some Blacks moved into the middle class, HBCUs continued to educate the majority of Blacks, since majority institutions refused to enroll them. After 1954, Blacks were slowly gaining entry into majority institutions, although it would take almost 20 years for any real movement to take place. In the 1980s and 1990s, majority institutions were under immense pressure to diversify, and consequently, they offered scholarships to high-achieving Black students, pulling them away from HBCUs that could not provide the same kind of funding. The "brain drain," as many sociologists called it, that took place at HBCUs caused many to believe that HBCUs only educate low-achieving students (Seymore, 2006).

To believe that HBCUs are irrelevant and contribute to student failure is to dismiss the complexity of American higher education. HBCUs recruit and educate a highly disproportionate number of students from the poor and middle class; 71% of HBCU students receive federal Pell grants (Gasman, 2013). It is no surprise that Black students, as well as Hispanics, on average, enter college more underprepared than their White and Asian peers (Kao & Thompson, 2003). Poverty, experienced within many Black communities, prevents many minority students from procuring the opportunities—quality secondary schools, extracurricular activities, and testing preparatory services, to name a few—needed to enter and succeed in college. Students choose to attend HBCUs due to curricular offerings, family legacy, or an interest in being educated in an environment that empowers them by providing same-race role models (Gasman et al., 2010). Given this, HBCUs are experienced in addressing this poverty and using it to transform underprepared students into accomplished and high-achieving graduates. Because HBCUs represent 3% of all postsecondary institutions in the United States and enroll 11% of all Black students, our nation and its policies cannot ignore the significance and contributions HBCUs have made to the higher education agenda (Gasman, 2013). In many instances, non-HBCUs are performing no better than HBCUs in graduating their students (Flores & Park, 2013). The performance of HBCUs and their ability to advance our nation's goals must be understood and compared appropriately to institutions with similar institutional structures and resources.

Unanswered Questions and Opportunities for Research

Historically Black colleges and universities have existed and played a part in the nation's development for the past three centuries. As they have evolved to reflect the social and economic trends during this time, the canon of literature and research on HBCUs to this day remains quite meager, yet ripe with untouched opportunity. Although we have touched on and addressed popular myths about HBCUs, we urge current and emerging researchers to develop sophisticated and innovative inquiries and studies in order to push and clarify our understanding of these complex communities. For instance:

- As HBCUs' student populations shift and grow to reflect the changing nation, how will leadership address the needs of these students?
- What can HBCU faculty teach faculty at other colleges and universities about teaching a diverse student body?
- As the country continues to embrace individuals who identify as LGBT, how will HBCUs lead discussions around advancing student inclusivity?

Some researchers might want to limit their research to institutions that are deemed popular or attached to a widely known legacy of success, educating and graduating the next generation of leaders. But it is equally important to pay heed to institutions—HBCUs—that continue to provide access to education to those whose communities have witnessed centuries of political, social, and economic oppression.

Conclusion

In the broadest sense, the term *historically Black colleges and universities* could be considered a misnomer. This designation has led society to take generally accepted notions of Blackness—racially segregated and homogeneous, heterosexual, Christian, poor, and unintelligent—to make sense of the culture and student populations of these very institutions. Based on our historical and contemporary review of the research on HBCUs, we know that these notions are simply false. But if one were to look into the historical representation of HBCUs, one would find that the designation is appropriate. It is important to remember that HBCUs emerged from a response to extreme and intentional exclusion of Blacks from established institutions that, to this day, continue to accrue and enjoy the patronage of the majority. This history is not one to be forgotten, but remembered and used to fuel the missions and policies of HBCUs to offer *all* students an opportunity of a quality education. A misnomer? We think not.

NEW DIRECTIONS FOR HIGHER EDUCATION • DOI: 10.1002/he

References

Anderson, J. A. (1997). Race, meritocracy, and the American academy during the immediate post–World War II era. *History of Education Quarterly*, *33*(2), 151–175.

Brown, L. K., Danovsky, M. B., Lourie, K. J., DiClemente, R. J., & Ponton, L. E. (1997). Adolescents with psychiatric disorders and the risk of HIV. *Journal of the American Academy of Child & Adolescent Psychiatry*, *36*(11), 1609–1617.

Brown, M. C., II, & Freeman, K. (Eds.). (2004). *Black colleges: New perspectives on policy and practice*. Westport, CT: Praeger.

Cohen, C. (1999). *The boundaries of Blackness: AIDS and the breakdown of Black politics*. Chicago, IL: University of Chicago Press.

Conrad, C., & Gasman, M. (2015). *Educating a diverse nation: Lessons from minority serving institutions*. Cambridge, MA: Harvard University Press.

Edgcomb, G. S. (1993). *From swastika to Jim Crow: Refugee scholars at Black colleges*. Malabar, FL: Krieger.

Flores, S. M., & Park, T. J. (2013). Race, ethnicity, and college success: Examining the continued significance of the minority-serving institution. *Educational Researcher*, *42*(3), 115–128.

Gasman, M. (1999). Scylla and Charybdis: Navigating the waters of academic freedom at Fisk University during Charles S. Johnson's administration (1946–1956). *American Educational Research Journal*, *36*(4), 739–758.

Gasman, M. (2001). Passport to the front of the bus: The impact of Fisk University's international program on race relations in Nashville, Tennessee. *49th Parallel—The International Journal of North American Studies*, *7*. Retrieved from http://repository .upenn.edu/gse_pubs/21/

Gasman, M. (2007). *Envisioning Black colleges: A history of the United Negro College Fund*. Baltimore, MD: Johns Hopkins University Press.

Gasman, M. (2013). *The changing face of historically Black colleges and universities*. Philadelphia, PA: Center for Minority Serving Institutions, University of Pennsylvania.

Gasman, M., Lundy-Wagner, V., Ransom, T., & Bowman, N., III. (2010). *Unearthing promise and potential: Our nation's historically Black colleges and universities*. San Francisco, CA: Jossey-Bass.

Gasman, M., & Tudico, C. (2008). *Historically Black colleges and universities: Triumphs, troubles, and taboos*. New York, NY: Palgrave.

Gilpin, P. J., & Gasman, M. (2003). *Charles S. Johnson: Leadership behind the veil in the age of Jim Crow*. Albany, NY: SUNY Press.

Harper, S. R., & Gasman, M. (2008). Consequences of conservatism: Black male undergraduates and the politics of historically Black colleges and universities. *The Journal of Negro Education*, *77*(4), 336–351.

Institute of Medicine. (2011). *The health of lesbian, gay, bisexual, and transgender people: Building a foundation for better understanding*. Washington, DC: Author.

Kao, G., & Thompson, J. S. (2003). Racial and ethnic stratification in educational achievement and attainment. *Annual Review of Sociology*, *29*, 417–442.

Karabel, J. (2006). *The chosen: The hidden history of admission and exclusion at Harvard, Yale, and Princeton*. Boston, MA: Mariner Books.

National Center for Education Statistics. (2011). *1980 fall enrollment at historically Black colleges and universities*. Integrated Postsecondary Education Data System (IPEDS). Washington, DC: U.S. Department of Education.

Nguyen, T., Samayoa, A. C., Mobley, S., & Gasman, M. (2014). *Challenging respectability: The case of student health centers at historically Black colleges and universities*. University of Pennsylvania. Manuscript submitted for publication.

Patton, L. D. (2011). Perspectives on identity, disclosure, and the campus environment among African American gay and bisexual men at one historically Black college. *Journal of College Student Development, 52*(1), 77–100.

Seymore, S. B. (2006). I'm confused: How can the federal government promote diversity in higher education yet continue to strengthen historically Black colleges? *Washington and Lee Journal of Civil Rights and Social Justice, 12*(2), 287–319.

Thompson, D. C. (1973). *Private Black colleges at the crossroads.* Westport, CT: Greenwood.

U.S. Census Bureau. (2011). *Overview of race and Hispanic origin: 2010.* Washington, DC: Author.

Williams, J., & Ashley, D. (2004). *I'll find a way or make one: A tribute to historically Black colleges and universities.* New York, NY: HarperCollins.

MARYBETH GASMAN *is a professor of higher education in the Graduate School of Education at the University of Pennsylvania.*

THAI-HUY NGUYEN *is a PhD candidate in higher education in the Graduate School of Education at the University of Pennsylvania.*

NEW DIRECTIONS FOR HIGHER EDUCATION • DOI: 10.1002/he

2

This chapter emphasizes the importance of going beyond racial and ethnic diversity at HBCUs to include other forms of diversity such as socioeconomic status, sexual orientation, and international status.

Moving Beyond Racial and Ethnic Diversity at HBCUs

John Michael Lee Jr.

In 2013, the U.S. Supreme Court heard the case of *Fisher v. University of Texas* concerning the affirmative action admissions policy of the University of Texas at Austin. This case, once again, brought the use of race-based admissions back to the forefront of American higher education. When the Supreme Court decided to void the lower appellate court's ruling in favor of the university and remand the case back to the lower courts, the justices argued that the lower court had not applied the standard of strict scrutiny that had been articulated by the Supreme Court in *Grutter v. Bollinger* (2003) and *Regents of the University of California v. Bakke* (1978).

While the Supreme Court's ruling in *Fisher* reaffirmed the constitutionality of using race as a factor in college admissions established in the cases of *Grutter* and *Bakke*, it has also continued to further the notion that diversity in the United States is only about race and ethnicity. The affirmative action policies that have been consistently used in higher education and challenged through the courts seek to remedy the vestiges of racism in the United States. Educators have consistently argued that affirmative action policies are justified because they ensure the creation of racially and ethnically diverse student bodies essential to providing students with the best possible education, and several studies have demonstrated that students who are exposed to engagement with diverse peers have seen enhanced educational outcomes (Gurin, Dey, Hurtado, & Gurin, 2002).

As the debate continues to play out about the value of diversity in mainstream higher education, there have been very few efforts to understand how diversity outcomes should be addressed at minority-serving institutions such as historically Black colleges and universities (HBCUs) (Dwyer, 2006). A parallel and related debate about the perceived lack of diversity at HBCUs continues to unfold. This debate is partially the result of the

New Directions for Higher Education, no. 170, Summer 2015 © 2015 Wiley Periodicals, Inc.
Published online in Wiley Online Library (wileyonlinelibrary.com) • DOI: 10.1002/he.20129

federal desegregation policies established in the middle of the 20th century in American higher education. Though the purpose of these policies was to end the segregation of institutions of higher education, it later resulted in a shift from promoting desegregation at predominantly White institutions (PWIs) to dismantling HBCUs (St. John & Musoba, 2003). Today, HBCUs continue to find themselves a topic of debate about whether they should exist in a post–*Brown v. Board of Education* and post-Obama environment. In addition, the relevancy of HBCUs has been the subject of academic inquiry, and many media outlets recently have raised questions about the continued existence of these institutions. Some believe that HBCUs are a remaining vestige of segregation (Allen & Jewell, 2002; Clay, 2013; Lee & Keys, 2013). Additionally, many also question the relevance of HBCUs now that African Americans have the ability to attend any institution of higher education of their choice.

HBCUs emerged as places to educate African Americans at a time when they could not attend PWIs by custom or by law (Roebuck & Murty, 1993), and many HBCU proponents believe that these institutions have already achieved diversity because they primarily serve African-American students. This notion held by many HBCU supporters provides a unique challenge to exploring broader topics of diversity at HBCUs. In fact, many see diversity as something that HBCUs are exempt from addressing because they have never excluded students on the basis of race or gender (Jewell, 2002). An overarching problem is that race and ethnicity have consistently been the sole prism by which the courts—and HBCUs—have traditionally approached the term *diversity* in these institutions.

This chapter examines data showing the diversity—broadly defined—that currently exists at HBCUs. This is followed by an examination of what the term *diversity* currently means and how this term can be redefined by HBCUs to move beyond the limitations of so-called structural diversity—that is, the numerical representation of racial/ethnic groups on a college or university campus (Hurtado, Milem, Clayton-Pedersen, & Allen, 1999). The chapter then describes what diversity means in the overall context of American higher education and makes the case for why current changes in American higher education will move HBCUs to embrace various forms of diversity. The chapter concludes with implications for research and practice at HBCUs.

Not Monolithic: Examining the Diversity of HBCUs

Examining diversity at HBCUs should start with a recognition that while they are a distinctive set of institutions that were created from humble beginnings and in a painful period of American history, today they are a collection of diverse college and universities that are a part of the 4,879 degree-granting 2-year and 4-year institutions in the United States (1,783 two-year and 3,096 four-year institutions). HBCUs make significant contributions to

Figure 2.1. Historically Black Colleges and Universities by Level, 2011

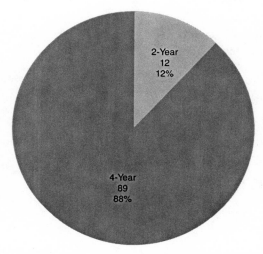

Source: National Center for Education Statistics, Integrated Postsecondary Education Data System (IPEDS), 2011. Data compiled by author.

student access and attainment, American research and innovation, and the national economy (Lee & Keys, 2013). In the United States today, there are currently 105 HBCUs, representing about 3% of higher education institutions in the country (Gasman, 2013). While the "HBCU" moniker readily identifies institutions with similar histories and missions, it does not capture the range of institutions that are included in this category. The majority of HBCUs (88%) are 4-year institutions (see Figure 2.1), and a little over half (51%) are public institutions (see Figure 2.2). Land-grant HBCUs (established under the Morrill Act of 1890) represent 17% of all HBCUs (Lee & Keys, 2013). HBCUs are represented in six distinct Carnegie Classifications (see Figure 2.3) that include research universities (10%), master's universities (24%), baccalaureate colleges and universities (48%), medical schools (2%), seminaries (4%), and associate-degree-granting institutions (12%).

Today's HBCUs represent a range of institutional types and sizes that offer students many majors and degrees. While some HBCUs, such as Tougaloo College and Spelman College, still offer students a primarily liberal arts education, others such as Florida A&M University, North Carolina A&T State University, and Howard University offer students a comprehensive selection of degrees and majors that include architecture, agriculture, engineering, and pharmacy. HBCUs also vary in the size of their student bodies. Table 2.1 shows the 10 HBCUs with the largest enrollments. While the average enrollment for all HBCUs is 3,393 students, Figure 2.4 shows HBCU enrollment differences by level, sector, and Carnegie Classification.

Figure 2.2. Historically Black Colleges and Universities by Sector, 2011

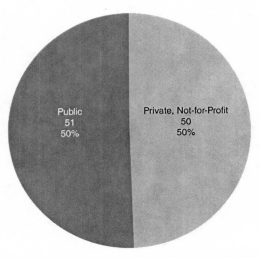

Source: National Center for Education Statistics, Integrated Postsecondary Education Data System (IPEDS), 2011. Data compiled by author.

Figure 2.3. Historically Black Colleges and Universities by Basic Carnegie Classification, 2011

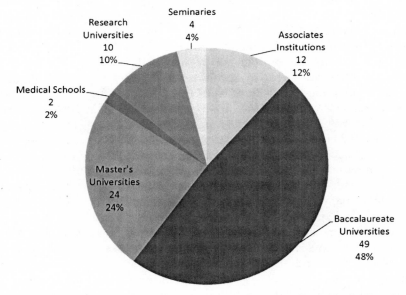

Source: National Center for Education Statistics, Integrated Postsecondary Education Data System (IPEDS), 2011. Data compiled by author.

Table 2.1. Top 10 Historically Black Colleges and Universities by Total Student Enrollment, 2011

Name of Institution	Enrollment
Florida Agricultural and Mechanical University (FAMU)	13,204
Hinds Community College	12,708
North Carolina A&T State University	10,881
St. Philip's College	10,710
Howard University	10,583
Texas Southern University	9,730
Tennessee State University	9,165
Jackson State University	8,903
Prairie View A&M University	8,425
North Carolina Central University	8,359

Source: National Center for Education Statistics, Integrated Postsecondary Education Data System (IPEDS), 2011.

Figure 2.4. Historically Black Colleges and Universities by Average Enrollment, 2011

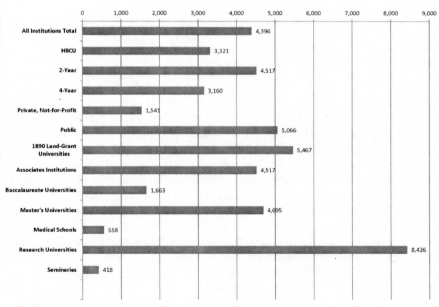

Note: "All Institutions" includes HBCUs and non-HBCUs. All other data are for HBCUs only.
Source: National Center for Education Statistics, Integrated Postsecondary Education Data System (IPEDS), 2011. Data compiled by author.

Figure 2.5. Historically Black Colleges and Universities by Degree Offering Status, 2011

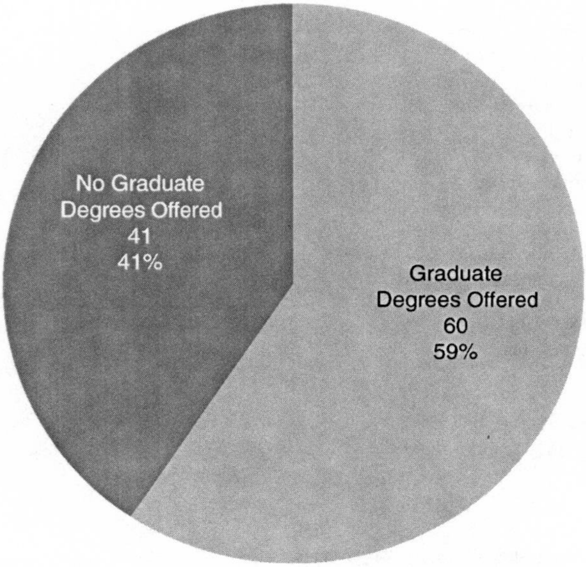

No Graduate
Degrees Offered
41
41%

Graduate
Degrees Offered
60
59%

Source: National Center for Education Statistics, Integrated Postsecondary Education Data System (IPEDS), 2011. Data compiled by author.

While most HBCUs primarily serve undergraduate students, 59% of them offer graduate or professional degrees as well (see Figure 2.5). The highest degrees offered at HBCUs vary greatly and include associate's degrees (12%), bachelor's degrees (33%), master's degrees (27%), and doctoral and professional degrees (28%) (see Figure 2.6).

Racial and Ethnic Diversity at HBCUs.   Overall HBCU enrollment has grown 42% over the past decade. HBCUs currently enroll 9% of all African-American students enrolled in U.S. higher education as well as other racially diverse students (Lee & Keys, 2013). Within HBCUs, 83% of students are African American, 13% are White, 3% are Hispanic, and 1% are Asian students (see Figure 2.7).

From 2000 to 2010, HBCUs more than doubled their enrollment of Asian students and increased Hispanic student enrollment by 90% and American Indian and White student enrollments by 56% and 55%, respectively (see Figure 2.8). Between 1970 and 2011, HBCUs have nearly doubled White student enrollment from 20,000 to nearly 40,000 (Lee & Keys, 2013). Graduate students at HBCUs are more racially and ethnically diverse than undergraduate students (Lee, 2012), and in recent years HBCUs have been able to attract larger numbers of White students and Asian students in high-demand master's, doctoral, and professional fields (Carter &

Figure 2.6. Historically Black Colleges and Universities by Highest Degree Offering, 2011

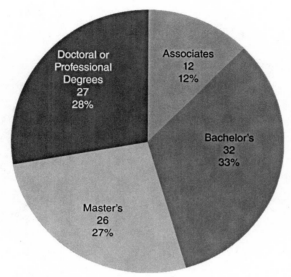

Source: National Center for Education Statistics, Integrated Postsecondary Education Data System (IPEDS), 2011. Data compiled by author.

Fountaine, 2012; Closson & Henry, 2008; Hall & Closson, 2005; Strayhorn, 2010).

These increases were promoted, in large part, by state and federal government mandates, as HBCUs in states such as Tennessee, North Carolina, and Mississippi were court ordered to improve racial imbalances. For example, court orders charged Tennessee State University to increase its non-Black enrollment by 50%, and similar benchmarks to increase diversity by 10% were placed on Alcorn State University, Jackson State University, and Mississippi Valley State University (Lee, 2011).

While court orders changed the makeup of some universities, other HBCUs saw significant changes in diversity because of the unique demographics of their state.

Both Bluefield State College and West Virginia State University saw predominantly African-American student enrollments change to predominantly White student enrollments because of the small numbers of African Americans in West Virginia. While today these institutions each have majority White student bodies, they still maintain their designation as HBCUs and continue their mission to provide access to African Americans within their new student demographics.

Racial and Ethnic Diversity in Sports at HBCUs. One of the most visible areas of the change in racial/ethnic diversity at HBCUs has come in

Figure 2.7. Students Enrolled at Historically Black Colleges and Universities by Race/Ethnicity, 2011

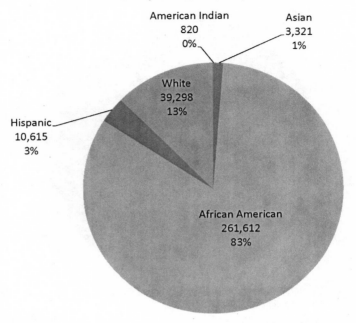

Source: National Center for Education Statistics, Integrated Postsecondary Education Data System (IPEDS), 2011. Data compiled by author.

the demographics of HBCU athletic teams. While HBCUs have traditionally never excluded groups of students, their sports programs have been populated overwhelmingly with African-American student athletes. This provided a competitive advantage for HBCUs before the 1970s, because talented Black athletes were not able to play sports at many PWIs. After the end of racial segregation and the eventual inclusion of African Americans in sports at PWIs, HBCUs sports teams have struggled to attract the same level of talent that existed during the segregation of college athletics. HBCU sports teams have found it hard to compete with other universities for the limited number of talented African-American athletes in many sports, and in many cases lack the financial resources to compete with other institutions.

In order to be more competitive in different sports, several HBCUs have recruited talent among non-African-American athletes. For example, the 2013–2014 women's bowling team at the University of Maryland Eastern Shore (UMES), which won the 2008, 2011, and 2012 National Collegiate Athletic Association (NCAA) National Championship in bowling and

Figure 2.8. Change in Fall Enrollments at Historically Black Colleges and Universities by Selected Characteristics, 2000–2010

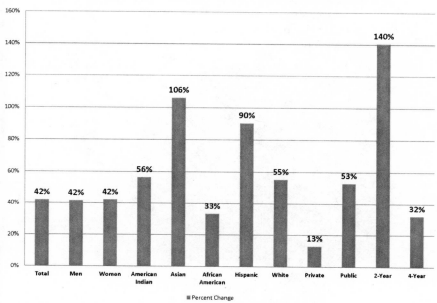

Source: National Center for Education Statistics, Integrated Postsecondary Education Data System (IPEDS), 2011. Data compiled by author.

is consistently one of the top bowling teams in the country, is predominantly White, as is the baseball team at Stillman College, a private HBCU in Alabama. Stillman's team won the Southern Intercollegiate Athletic Conference (SIAC) baseball championship each year from 2007 to 2014.

HBCUs are increasingly diversifying their student bodies through sports, and many of the successes that some HBCUs have experienced in athletics can be directly attributed to changes in their recruitment strategies. HBCU marching bands have even started to attract non-Black musicians. Interestingly, while some HBCUs are increasing racial and ethnic diversity of student athletes, other HBCUs pride themselves on remaining purists by fielding only African-American athletic teams. This mind-set presents a challenge to increasing diversity in HBCU athletics.

Faculty Diversity at HBCUs.   Diversity at HBCUs is not confined to diversity among students. Faculty diversity is also important. While concerns about faculty diversity have mainly focused on PWIs, HBCUs are also concerned about this issue. Data from the National Center for Education Statistics (NCES) show that as of 2011 most faculty at all 4-year institutions are White (79%), yet there are also small percentages of Asian (8%),

Figure 2.9. Faculty at All Degree-Granting 4-Year Institutions by Race/Ethnicity, 2011

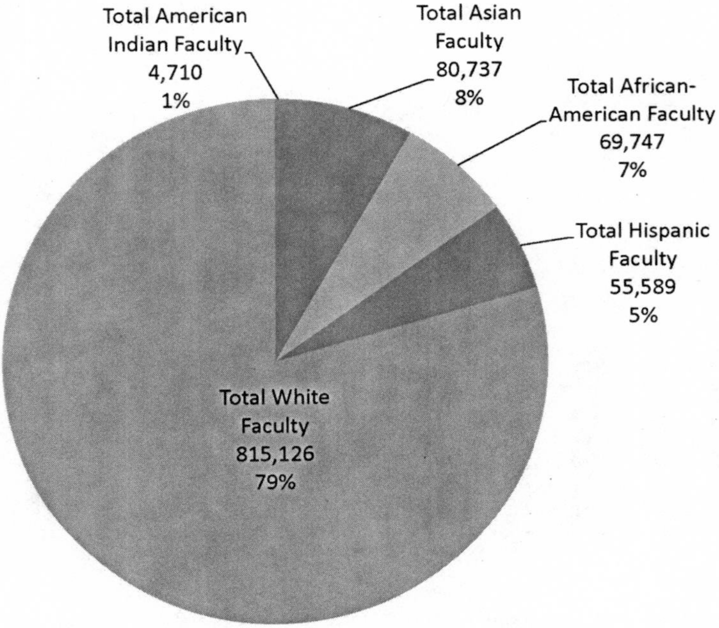

Total American Indian Faculty
4,710
1%

Total Asian Faculty
80,737
8%

Total African-American Faculty
69,747
7%

Total Hispanic Faculty
55,589
5%

Total White Faculty
815,126
79%

Source: National Center for Education Statistics, Integrated Postsecondary Education Data System (IPEDS), 2011. Data compiled by author.

African-American (7%), Hispanic (5%), and American Indian (1%) faculty at 4-year colleges and universities (see Figure 2.9). The current racial and ethnic makeup of faculty at American colleges and universities does not yet mirror existing student diversity. While faculty diversity at all colleges and universities continues to be a concern, HBCU faculties are significantly more diverse than their counterparts at PWIs. Figure 2.10 shows that while 63% of faculty members at HBCUs are African-American, an additional 26% are White, 9% are Asian, and 2% are Hispanic.

(Re)Framing Diversity

Structural diversity is the numerical representation of racial/ethnic groups on a college or university campus (Hurtado et al., 1999). While it is easy to define structural diversity, it is much harder to determine when it has been accomplished. Is an institution that is 75% White and 25% non-White more or less diverse than a school that is 80% African-American and 20% non-African-American or a school that is 75% Latino and 25% non-Latino? The

Figure 2.10.   Faculty at Degree-Granting 4-Year Historically Black Colleges and Universities by Race/Ethnicity, 2011

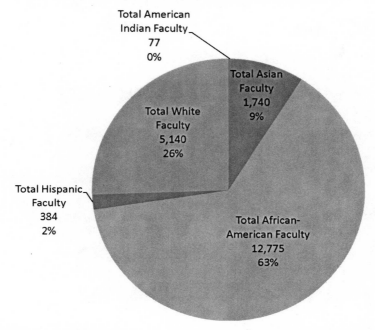

Source: National Center for Education Statistics, Integrated Postsecondary Education Data System (IPEDS), 2011. Data compiled by author.

answers really depend on the broader context of the institution and the goals of diversity that have been set. One of the most daunting limitations of focusing only on the structural aspects of diversity is that institutions do not take into account the various elements that extend beyond race and ethnicity. These other elements are important to expanding diversity and inclusion at HBCUs beyond dimensions of structural racial and ethnic diversity. The following subsections explore socioeconomic diversity, diversity as it relates to sexual orientation, and internationalization.

Socioeconomic Diversity at HBCUs. The mission of HBCUs—to provide education to those who would not normally have access to college—has led to significant socioeconomic diversity among HBCU students. One of the ways to measure this diversity is to look at the number of students receiving federal Pell grants and student loans. The National Center for Education Statistics reports that in 2011, 49% of students at all institutions were receiving Pell grants; at HBCUs 71% of students were Pell recipients (see Figure 2.11). Similarly, NCES reported that 54% all undergraduate students received federal loans, and this figure was significantly

Figure 2.11. Percentage of Students Receiving Pell Grants at Historically Black Colleges and Universities by Selected Characteristics, 2011

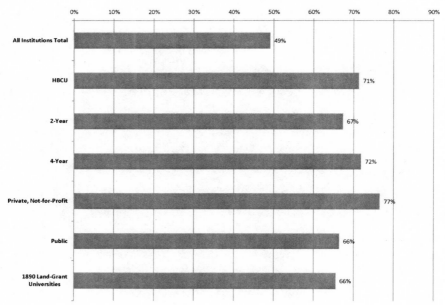

Note: "All Institutions" includes HBCUs and non-HBCUs. All other data are for HBCUs only.
Source: National Center for Education Statistics, Integrated Postsecondary Education Data System (IPEDS), 2011. Data compiled by author.

higher at HBCUs (71%) (see Figure 2.12). These data show that HBCUs are socioeconomically diverse and provide significant access for low-income students.

Lesbian, Gay, Bisexual, and Transgender Diversity at HBCUs. It is important as we look to redefine diversity at HBCUs beyond the historical context of race and ethnicity that we also consider lesbian, gay, bisexual, and transgender (LGBT) diversity. Historically, HBCUs have not been ideal places for individuals who have identified themselves as LGBT. As the nation and many other institutions and organizations have become more accepting of individuals who identify as LGBT, HBCUs have responded to this population at a much slower pace (Harper & Gasman, 2008). HBCUs have traditionally fostered conservative religious environments that have been restrictive for LGBT students, and this puts HBCUs at a competitive disadvantage to other institutions that have more tolerance and support for these students. As American culture changes to be more accepting of individuals who are a part of the LGBT community—both legally and socially—HBCUs must also become part of this change.

NEW DIRECTIONS FOR HIGHER EDUCATION • DOI: 10.1002/he

Figure 2.12. Percentage of Students Receiving Federal Loans at Historically Black Colleges and Universities by Selected Characteristics, 2011

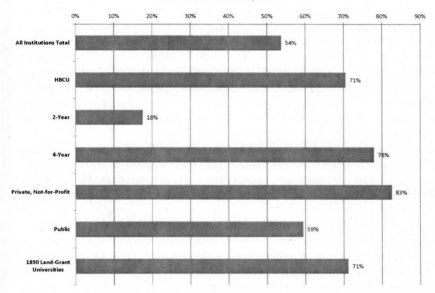

Note: "All Institutions" includes HBCUs and non-HBCUs. All other data are for HBCUs only.
Source: National Center for Education Statistics, Integrated Postsecondary Education Data System (IPEDS), 2011. Data compiled by author.

This is not to say that nothing is being done; according to Gasman (2013), there are 21 HBCUs that currently have LGBT student organizations. For example, Florida A&M University has an LGBT Student Pride Union that serves as a safe space for LGBT students and those who support them. In addition to offering student organizations, many HBCUs are also developing academic programs and course work in an effort not only to educate the student populations on these issues but also to increase the diversity of their institutions through knowledge and empowerment.

While institutions can ensure that LGBT students have a sense of community through organizations and that they have access to courses on LGBT issues, HBCUs must also foster supportive environments across the entire campus. For example, Alcorn State University sought to build a diverse and inclusive environment throughout the entire campus for LGBT students by bringing the first gay couple to be featured in *Jet* magazine's wedding profiles to lecture at the campus in 2013. This effort to promote a diverse and inclusive environment was met with resistance from both citizens and alumni. Despite this opposition—or perhaps because of it—HBCUs must do more to promote inclusive environments.

The Internationalization of HBCUs.   HBCUs are not only embracing socioeconomic diversity and LGBT diversity, but they are also attracting more international students. More international students attended HBCUs in the 1990s than attend today; therefore, HBCUs are renewing efforts to strategically attract international students back to HBCU campuses. In 1994, 6,069 international students were enrolled at HBCUs (2% of all students who were enrolled at HBCUs in 1994) compared to only 5,549 international students enrolled in 2012. However, more than 12% of students at land-grant HBCUs are from foreign countries (Lee & Keys, 2013), and the 18 land-grant HBCUs educate over 1,200 students from foreign countries, including China, Brazil, and Ghana (Association of Public and Land-Grant Universities, 2013).

HBCUs have been increasing the number of agreements with foreign governments to attract and enroll international students and are participating in strategic government initiatives to increase diversity. For example, HBCUs are a part of the U.S. Department of State's HBCU & Brazilian Universities Exchange whereby Brazilian students are studying English, teacher education, and communication at HBCUs across the United States. This alliance has brought more than 150 Brazilian students to the United States for fully funded study at more than 15 HBCUs. Similarly, HBCUs such as North Carolina A&T State University and Delaware State University have implemented initiatives to bring more international students to their campuses to ensure that their students have access to an education that prepares them to work in a global economy. More HBCUs must create initiatives to ensure that their students are competitive in a global economy, and this can happen only when HBCUs build environments where students are exposed to diversity through many different lenses.

While three types of nonstructural diversity have been mentioned, diversity should not be limited to these areas alone and should be inclusive rather than exclusive.

Changes in Higher Education Affecting HBCUs

The rapid pace of change in higher education affects colleges and universities at all levels as performance measures move away from inputs such as the number of students, faculty, facilities, and programs toward outcome metrics that include retention and graduation, postgraduation outcomes (e.g., employment, enrollment in graduate school), and the production of career-ready graduates. Figure 2.13 shows the various pressures that are challenging every institution in the nation (including HBCUs) regardless of their types, characteristics, or student differences. No college or university can ignore these challenges, especially those such as HBCUs that have limited resources and serve primarily low-income and minority students, because these institutions will feel a disproportionate impact of these changes.

NEW DIRECTIONS FOR HIGHER EDUCATION • DOI: 10.1002/he

Figure 2.13. The Changing Landscape of Higher Education

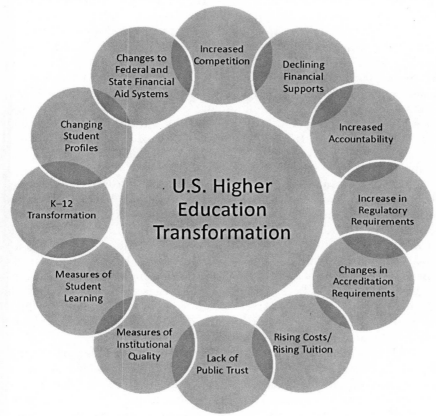

Source: Association of Public and Land-Grant Universities, 2013.

The Increased Competition for African-American Students. Due to the decreasing and limited resources at both public and private institutions, the competition among them has increased for both resources and students. African-American students are now in an environment where not only can they go to any institution legally, but also they are being welcomed, actively recruited, and financially enticed to enroll by colleges and universities where they would not have been admissible 50 years ago. The growth of African-American enrollments at institutions such as Georgia State University, the University of Southern Mississippi, Florida State University, the University of North Carolina–Greensboro, and similar institutions should not be overlooked. As enrollment options for African-American students increase, HBCUs find themselves in a different and more competitive environment. They must confront this new competition while continuing to navigate historical challenges and threats that have long existed.

HBCUs are experiencing declining enrollments, financial exigency, and continued questions about their long-term viability. In this environment, HBCUs are searching for new and innovative ways to replace declining financial support from federal, state, and local sources and find new strategies for improving student outcomes that will be tied to state and federal funding for higher education. While many states already link appropriations for HBCUs to performance on student outcome metrics, President Barack Obama's new higher education agenda seeks the establishment of a college rating system that will link federal funding to student performance. HBCUs have been highly criticized for their graduation rates that are on average about 30% (Gasman, 2013) and must chart a new course if they are to survive myriad changes and the danger of being eradicated as an institutional sector.

The Case for Increased Diversity at HBCUs.   HBCU enrollments are shrinking among African-American students while predominantly White institutions, community colleges, and for-profit institutions are seeing record growth in African-American student enrollment. In 2005, 20% of African-American students in American higher education were enrolled in HBCUs compared to only 9% today (Lee & Keys, 2013). HBCU enrollments will not be sustainable if they singularly recruit and enroll African-American students. HBCUs must become more diverse because of the short supply of adequately prepared African-American students in the academic pipeline, the increased competition for African-American students among all institutional types, and the changing demographics for the country.

As HBCUs respond to the changing demographics and demand of students in U.S. higher education, many questions must be addressed. How will increased diversity affect the HBCU climate and culture? What infrastructures are needed for HBCUs to welcome diverse students to the campus? What are the best ways for HBCUs to attract diverse students? What are the benefits or the adverse effects to HBCUs from increasing diversity? HBCUs must also understand the financial and human resource implications of developing diverse student bodies. Will HBCUs need to hire diverse recruiters to recruit diverse students? How can this sector improve the way HBCUs are currently viewed in the United States?

The economic case being made for the further diversification of HBCUs is not rooted in a view that HBCUs lack diversity. In fact, they are, in many ways, more diverse than many PWIs and provide opportunities for underserved students who are not currently participating in other sectors of American higher education. Simply put, HBCUs are access centers for diverse students in terms of race/ethnicity, socioeconomic, first-generation, or international status. Increasing diversity at HBCUs is more than simply increasing the number of White students or denying access to some Black students who are currently being served at these institutions. HBCUs should think strategically about diversity in the HBCU context and what other students they can serve. For example, some institutions may decide to reach out to the growing Hispanic student population that will be a major part of the coming demographic change in the United States, while other institutions may reach out to low-income and first-generation students of all races that mirror the students who currently attend HBCUs. HBCUs may also consider attracting more international students—especially those from Africa and Latin America—who can add diverse learning experiences to the HBCU environment.

Increasing diversity at HBCUs should be a strategic exercise. They can become centers of access and opportunity for all students and still maintain their focus and culture as HBCUs. This is the power of the proverbial *and* instead of the dichotomous *or*. While HBCU proponents might argue that this would drastically alter the culture of HBCUs, not making this change will permanently alter the landscape of HBCUs because it will mean the closure or merger of some institutions. While some HBCUs are moving aggressively to attract, and create supportive environments for, diverse and foreign students, most HBCUs have not made the changes necessary to prepare for the students of tomorrow.

Implications for Future Research and Practice at HBCUs

Exploring diversity at HBCUs is a topic that must be examined and reexamined through many different lenses. As we seek to redefine what diversity means within the HBCU space, future research will have to explore the not-so-obvious aspects of diversity at HBCUs. It is evident through the data presented within this chapter that diversity on these campuses extends beyond having more than one racial or ethnic group on a campus. Diversity also extends to the socioeconomic background, sexual identity, and international identity of students, and yet diversity is not limited to these three categories.

We must seek new forms of diversity at HBCUs and find other ways to quantify this diversity. While redefining diversity in the HBCU context should be a goal of future research and practice, it will also be important to further examine racial and ethnic diversity at HBCUs and the effects of increased diversity on the HBCU mission, culture, and students. HBCU researchers and practitioners must push the boundaries of diversity and reframe it to move beyond racial/ethnic remedies to the solution for preparing students who can compete in a global society. This removes the lens of diversity as only a remedy for segregation—a lens that prohibits HBCUs from seeing the role they can play in redefining diversity.

HBCU practitioners must also recognize that the higher education landscape is changing dramatically, and that they will not survive these changes without embracing diversity. HBCUs must embrace diversity not only to ensure their survival, but also to attract the students of tomorrow who see diversity as a key to success in society. Many potential students do not consider HBCUs as an educational option because they do not believe that broad societal diversity exists on these campuses. HBCUs must change this narrative not only to compete for African-American students but also to encourage other groups of students to attend their institutions.

When HBCUs truly become serious about recruiting diverse students, they will need to expand their recruitment and admission staffs to include diverse individuals as well. How can an HBCU be truly committed to increasing the number of Latino students on its campus without individuals on the campus in key areas who speak Spanish, understand Spanish culture, and are willing to create spaces on campus for Hispanic students to thrive? The same is true if HBCUs are serious about recruiting Native American, Asian, White, and international students. HBCUs must equip themselves with a diverse workforce—both faculty and staff—if they expect to recruit the students of the future. HBCUs would then be positioned to recruit non-African-American students who would be attracted to HBCUs in order to be taught by the most diverse faculty in academia. HBCUs can move beyond the limitations of racial/ethnic diversity in the United States and create a new vision for diversity in American higher education.

References

Allen, W. R., & Jewell, J. O. (2002). A backward glance forward: Past, present, and future perspectives on historically Black colleges and universities. *Review of Higher Education, 25*(3), 241–261.

Association of Public and Land-Grant Universities. (2013). *1890 teaching, research, and innovation award survey*. Washington, DC: Author.

Carter, J. D., & Fountaine, T. P. (2012). An analysis of White student engagement at public HBCUs. *Educational Foundations, 26*(3), 49–66.

Clay, P. L. (2013). *Historically Black colleges and universities: Facing the future; A fresh look at challenges and opportunities*. Ford Foundation working paper. Cambridge, MA: Massachusetts Institute of Technology.

Closson, R. B., & Henry, W. J. (2008). Racial and ethnic diversity at HBCUs: What can be learned when Whites are in the minority? *Multicultural Education, 15*(4), 15–19.

Dwyer, B. (2006). Framing the effect of multiculturalism on diversity outcomes among students at historically Black colleges and universities. *Educational Foundations,* Winter–Spring, 37–59.

Gasman, M. (2013). *The changing face of historically Black colleges and universities*. Philadelphia, PA: Center for Minority Serving Institutions, University of Pennsylvania.

Grutter v. Bollinger, 539 U.S. 306 (2003).

Gurin, P., Dey, E. L., Hurtado, S., & Gurin, G. (2002). Diversity and higher education: Theory and impact on educational outcomes. *Harvard Educational Review, 72*(3), 330–366.

Hall, B., & Closson, R. (2005). When the majority is the minority: White graduate students social adjustment at an HBCU. *Journal of College Student Development, 46*(1), 28–41.

Harper, S. R., & Gasman, M. (2008). Consequences of conservatism: Black male undergraduates and the politics of historically Black colleges and universities. *The Journal of Negro Education, 77*(4), 336–351.

Hurtado, S., Milem, J., Clayton-Pedersen, A., & Allen, W. (1999). *Enacting diverse learning environments: Improving the climate for racial/ethnic diversity in higher education* [ASHE-ERIC Higher Education Report, 26(8)]. Washington, DC: George Washington University, Graduate School of Education and Human Development.

Jewell, J. O. (2002). To set an example: The tradition of diversity at historically Black colleges and universities. *Urban Education, 37*(1), 7–21.

Lee, J. M., Jr. (2011). *American higher education without public HBCUs.* New York, NY: Lambert Academic Publishing.

Lee, J. M., Jr. (2012). African American graduate education at HBCUs: Trends, experiences and outcomes. In R. T. Palmer, A. Hilton, & T. Fountaine (Eds.), *Black graduate education at historically Black colleges and universities: Trends, experiences, and outcomes* (pp. 61–83). London, UK: Information Age Press.

Lee, J. M., Jr., & Keys, S. W. (2013). *Repositioning HBCUs for the future: Access, success, research & innovation.* Office for Access and Success Discussion Paper 2013-01. Washington, DC: Association of Public and Land-Grant Universities.

Regents of the University of California v. Bakke, 438 U.S. 265 (1978).

Roebuck, J., & Murty, K. (1993). *Historically Black colleges and universities: Their place in American higher education.* Westport, CT: Praeger.

St. John, E. P., & Musoba, G. D. (2003). Academic access and equal opportunity: Rethinking the foundations for policy on diversity. *Equity and access in higher education: Changing the definition of educational opportunity—Readings on equal education, 18.*

Strayhorn, T. L. (2010). Majority as temporary minority: Examining the influence of faculty-student relationships on satisfaction among White undergraduates at historically Black colleges and universities. *Journal of College Student Development, 51*(5), 509–524.

JOHN MICHAEL LEE JR. is the vice president for the Office of Access and Success (OAS) at the Association for Public and Land-Grant Universities in Washington, DC.

3

Using narratives from a diverse group of students and staff in terms of race and religion, this chapter gives voice to these individuals' experiences with issues of diversity and inclusion at an HBCU. This chapter also discusses how these experiences helped to facilitate the authors' racial and cultural identity development.

HBCUs as Critical Context for Identity Work: Reflections, Experiences, and Lessons Learned

Derek F. Greenfield, Tony Innouvong, Richard Jay Aglugub, Ismail A. Yusuf

While tremendous attention has been placed on the importance of diversity within higher education in recent years, the dominant discourse in the scholarship primarily addresses the need for predominantly White institutions (PWIs) to become more receptive and inclusive for students of color. Clearly, this goal can be seen as laudable. But in essence, the limited focus serves to reify assimilationist and majoritarian paradigms that position PWIs at the cultural center and ignore the considerable efforts around diversity taking place at historically Black colleges and universities (HBCUs). Whether presuming that HBCUs are already diverse because they have large numbers of Black students or conversely not diverse under the erroneous assumption that non-Blacks are not welcomed, the narrative fails to appreciate the historical openness of HBCUs and the rich context available for gaining insights into the complexity of diversity work.

In particular, this chapter suggests that HBCUs offer diverse individuals a unique milieu for critically interrogating their own racial identities. With the historical mission in pursuit of social justice as well as supportive campus climate (McMickens, 2012), HBCUs typically deliver an environment conducive for this reflective self-examination. Indeed, the inverted cultural space privileging African-American cultural identities and traditions may challenge other-race groups of students to engage in these identity projects by positioning their realities in nonnormative fashion.

In spite of this backdrop, limited work has thoroughly examined the identity experiences of non-Blacks at HBCUs, with the vast majority

NEW DIRECTIONS FOR HIGHER EDUCATION, no. 170, Summer 2015 © 2015 Wiley Periodicals, Inc.
Published online in Wiley Online Library (wileyonlinelibrary.com) • DOI: 10.1002/he.20130

investigating White students. For example, Closson and Henry (2008) as well as Peterson and Hamrick (2009) argue that White students at HBCUs can benefit in terms of receiving an opportunity to examine Whiteness through a majority–minority situation and become potential allies in the mission for social justice. More recently, Palmer and Maramba (in press) address specific challenges facing "minority minorities" such as Asian Americans and Latino/as at HBCUs, identifying the presence of microaggressions that may hamper their social and educational outcomes.

Thus, there remains a need for richer understanding of diverse students' experiences at HBCUs, particularly regarding how racial identity may be impacted throughout their journey. As Hall (1997) asserts, identities are multiple, contested, and always in the process of becoming. By studying how these identities are negotiated and transacted within the HBCU context through detailed reflective narrative, the coauthors here hope to stimulate a new avenue of inquiry.

Theoretical and Methodological Orientation

In this chapter, we draw from several theoretical contributions. First, the symbolic interactionist paradigm is instrumental, as Blumer (1969) writes that through encounters with others and our own reflections of them, we make meaning of the world and come to develop a sense of self. With regard to race, these interactions within our racial group and outside shape how we assign meaning to our race-oriented experiences and influence the way we define the self through the prism of race.

Stryker's (1980) thinking on identity salience broadens the discussion of symbolic interactionism by suggesting that individuals create their own internal hierarchies of identity. Yet, it is important to note that contextual factors can influence the perceived salience of particular identities (Ellemers, Spears, & Doosje, 2002), in terms of how individuals evaluate their own positionality relative to the environment and how others respond in ways that highlight certain identities. Different contexts and audiences generate distinctive identity salience schemas.

While not specifically addressing formation of racial identity per se, it is our intention to examine how engagement within a particular social milieu can (re)shape one's understanding of race. Building from distinctiveness theory, individuals typically grant greater salience to identity features diverging significantly from others in that social environment (McGuire, McGuire, Child, & Fujioka, 1978). Clearly, at an HBCU, those who are non-Black may experience their race as a more salient identity marker for them, with heightened consciousness around social interactions.

Indeed, non-Black students entering HBCU institutions are often attempting to operate simultaneously within disparate racialized worlds. Anzaldua (1987) regards this interstitial reality as constituting a "borderlands" reality, with individuals being compelled to manage competing social identities. However, rather than conceptualizing this borderlands situation as inexorably problematic, she contends that affirming and internalizing a border identity offers a unique epistemological and ontological standpoint from which to better "recognize" the self and other. Anzaldua advances a four-stage model to describe this journey, illustrating how individuals immersed within settings as the "other" come to interrogate their own identities, appreciate the contextual nature of identity development, wrestle with often competing ways of being, and ultimately, in the final stage, assert a more blended identity to "operate in a pluralistic mode" (pp. 82–83).

It is our contention that diverse students at HBCUs may progress through similar stages. For example, a White student could plausibly not only gain insight into Whiteness and elements of privilege, but also discover the importance of adopting more inclusive belief systems while endeavoring to become an active ally for others. In reflecting on his "beautiful experience" at an HBCU, one White student commented, "Not only did I get an academic education, I got a cultural education. ... I don't believe I would have gotten that anywhere else" (Thomas-Lester, 2004, p. C01).

Building from the phenomenological approaches articulated in our theoretical framework, we incorporate autoethnography as a vehicle for sharing our stories and utilizing these reflections to produce greater understanding of the HBCU context. Ellis, Adams, and Bochner (2011) present autoethnography as an "approach to research and writing that seeks to describe and systematically analyze personal experience in order to understand cultural experience" (p. 1).

To be clear, the narratives explored in this chapter speak to the realities encountered at one HBCU. While not attempting to suggest complete generalizability (especially considering the tremendous variability in HBCU schools), the authors highlight aspects that could find resonance in the overall category of HBCUs. The site for this work is a Southern regional HBCU (pseudonym of Cedar State University) where the president had made a concerted effort to promote diversity and inclusion.

Our Stories

In this section, we discuss our stories.

Derek's Reflections.   Having worked at other HBCUs, and spending much of my personal and professional life in spaces promoting discourse around racial issues, I felt as if I had made significant progress in my racial identity journey when I entered Cedar State University. I would soon discover that the particular dynamics of being the university's first diversity director—and being a White male outsider to the institution and the state—created an intriguing framework for deeper reflection on racial identity and the performance of the racialized self.

New Directions for Higher Education • DOI: 10.1002/he

Throughout my time at Cedar State, I frequently heard comments viewing my presentation of self as indicative of a symbolic transracial identity. By presenting what were deemed "Black" cultural styles in an authentic manner, I was often racially coded as "Black," symbolized in statements such as "You're just a light-skinned brother." To be clear, I appreciated the positive sentiment but was not seeking to be a racial perpetrator.

As a result of this acceptance, I felt fairly comfortable navigating within areas of race in our office's work. Yet, interestingly enough, the greater challenges were faced when confronting other domains of diversity. For instance, progressive discussions of lesbian, gay, bisexual, and transgender (LGBT) issues or religious inclusion were not easily welcomed in our rural and largely Southern Baptist community, particularly among staff and alumni who may have been additionally concerned about the notion of a White male outsider sparking these conversations. My Whiteness then became more salient and imbued with a very different meaning, seemingly as a marker of efforts to move people unwillingly against their religious and heteronormative privilege.

Thus, in some ways, it eventually became less about how I performed, but rather how the very presence of Whiteness constituted a performance. While I could engage in culturally appropriate impression management to demonstrate my commitment as an ally and partner in the equality struggle, there were moments in which being a White male automatically performed for me a reality over which I held little control.

As an example, toward the end of my first year, a White male emerged as the leading candidate to serve as the head football coach. During a called meeting of leaders from various constituent groups, several older Black male alumni expressed concern about the notion of a White man filling the position. Referencing their own internal pain of being rejected for opportunities throughout their lives because of race, these individuals spoke openly about the importance of hiring a "real HBCU person." With a palpable tension enveloping the room, I moved to comment about expanding the definition of a "real HBCU person." Yet, before any words could be uttered, a senior administrator placed his hand over my arm and signaled for me to remain quiet. Initially frustrated by this silencing gesture, I ultimately appreciated the value of the move.

At that moment, my comments would have represented a patronizing invocation of racial privilege since these men needed to express those words publicly and have their realities acknowledged. Soon thereafter, several folks spoke powerfully about their own positive interactions with this coach and the desire to move the institution forward as an example of diversity. Indeed, for the very reason that these men had experienced outright racism, the speakers asserted that our school could model the spirit of inclusion for others by hiring the best candidate. Perhaps most poignantly, two students offered testimonies about coming to celebrate the importance of diversity through our office's work and wanting their beloved institution to not be held back by the trauma of the past.

Typically, members of privileged groups are not confronted with situations where their identities are considered problematic and questionable. Determining how to navigate this racial performance—especially with its personal and professional implications—became instructive for me. While psychologically taxing at times, it served as a reminder of how diversity work challenges individuals to confront a range of affective and cognitive issues that can be anxiety-producing.

As a result, I am thinking more intensely about the role of an ally within the context of Whiteness. Too often, allies simply lay claim to this position in an ironic act of privilege without obtaining guidance from those they purport to support. For pragmatic and even performative purposes, the dynamics and presentation of allyship need to be examined in greater depth—and my latest HBCU journey stimulated this process that is inextricably tied to matters of my own racial identity.

Tony's Reflections.   "Where are you from? No, where are you *really* from? What's your real name? Do you speak Asian? English? Do you know kung fu?" This is just a snapshot of the questions I was asked when I enrolled at Cedar State. I am an Asian American from Seattle of Lao descent who grew up speaking both Lao and English. I do not know any kung fu, but at Cedar State, I was as close as kung fu gets and was crowned the prestigious, exotic "First Asian Friend" on several occasions. While my instinct automatically revved up to take offense, I learned to seize the golden opportunity of sharing my story and history. But the names, comments, and questions were all forms of racial microaggressions that served as a constant reminder of my otherness and foreigner status. Though born on American soil, at times I can relate to Takaki's (1998) conceptualization of Asians as the perpetual foreigner, for I am frequently treated like a stranger from a different shore. I have always lived in two different worlds, but the world in which I was immersed at an HBCU was particularly challenging as a non-Black minority student.

I happen to be one of the relatively small number of Asian Americans, and quite possibly the only Lao American, enrolled at an HBCU. As a demographic outlier, it was only natural for me to be asked questions about who I was and why I was there. People inquired about my race and nationality, and often made the presumption that I was not "American." Questions and comments hinting at my "immigrant" status reinforced the subconscious notion that I was "foreign" and created alienation. My work in the Office of Diversity and involvement on campus ironically further exacerbated this feeling, as I became more visible and susceptible to people's curiosity. Addressing my race and nationality became as ingrained in my daily routine as my morning coffee.

New Directions for Higher Education • DOI: 10.1002/he

Unlike my ability to blend into the racially diverse and progressive environment of Seattle, the hypervisibility I experienced at Cedar State encouraged me to think more about my own racial identity, and ultimately led me to challenge problematic issues on campus. Being in a new cultural space, I found myself doing much more soul searching and even started asking my mom additional questions about our family history, both for myself and to spread knowledge to others at Cedar State. Questions on campus thus became opportunities to teach, so when asked, I answered. To cope with the change in environment, I constructed a strategy to creatively interact by joking along as a bridge to later sharing information and stories. And later, I became president of the International Student Organization to build community and promote cross-cultural awareness.

Reflecting on my experiences, I learned three important skills regarding race work at Cedar State: how to embrace the temporal discomfort of my visibility and view my uniqueness as advantageous in relationship building with others and myself; how to creatively challenge microaggressions, using them as stepping stones of enlightenment; and how to divert ethnocentricity to best inclusively represent the communities I identify with. The combination of all three taught me to think more critically about my identity and allowed me to more intentionally develop a much richer understanding of myself than I ever had done before.

My multidimensional experience at Cedar State has been pivotal in helping clarify the ambiguity chained to my racial identity. Despite the emotional hardship of maneuvering my otherness in an environment nearly opposite to what I consider home, I have grown a greater appreciation for culture and who I am as an Asian American as a result of my transition from Seattle to Cedar State.

Richard's Reflections.   I was born on O'ahu, Hawai'i, of Philippine immigrants, making me a first-generation Filipino American. In Hawai'i, phenotypical differences matter far less than cultural differences, as Filipinos are subject to a lot of ethnoracial discrimination. Our dress, language, and accents are mocked, and we are overrepresented in low socioeconomic status. This stigma leads Filipinos in Hawai'i to grow up feeling ashamed of their ethnic heritage. As a result, Filipino Americans create and assimilate to a pseudo-culture of "being local" and internally distance themselves from their heritage. I noticed that I constantly identified myself as being from Hawai'i, rather than Filipino, when arriving at Cedar State.

The intersecting cultures of the American South and of HBCU life were foreign to me. Upon matriculation, I instantly felt the need to assimilate into this new culture to gain social acceptance. There were also so many times when I was asked if I worked at the local Chinese restaurant or innocently called Mexican. With the frequent false assumptions made about my ethnicity, I desired to teach others about being Filipino American and from Hawai'i—yet I did not always act on this. Self-hate and even fear of nonacceptance were real.

NEW DIRECTIONS FOR HIGHER EDUCATION • DOI: 10.1002/he

While cultural assimilation usually makes people forget their identity, ironically my assimilation to HBCU life and the South ultimately encouraged me to better understand my own racial identity. Growing up in the diverse state of Hawai'i, I never had to explain what it means to be Filipino. Being at Cedar State, where I am the only full Filipino on campus, challenged me to confront my own identity in new ways. People wanted to know me, and I needed to know myself.

On November 8, 2013, Typhoon Haiyan, one of the deadliest tropical cyclones in history, struck the Philippines. As a first-generation Filipino American, I have only visited my mother's homeland a few times, but my heart broke at that moment. I could not fathom how my family members and friends born there were feeling, pain made worse when I thought that I had nobody at school to talk to about the tragedy shocking the entire Filipino diaspora.

Interestingly, when watching a professional football game with friends at Cedar State, I saw a player named Doug Baldwin run out onto the field waving the Philippine flag to draw attention to the crisis. It was the perfect opportunity to open up and offer my peers a piece of not only my mind, but of my roots and culture as well. From their positive response and my own satisfaction, I made it a point to strengthen my understanding of my ethnic identity, express my pride in being Filipino, and share it all to better learn about other people's cultures in return. You see, I too have a Philippine flag hanging on my dorm room wall above my bed. I am now honored to run onto the field as well.

Growing up a first-generation Filipino American in Hawai'i with limited opportunities, I not only saw my past and my heritage as a wasteland, but viewed my future as one as well. I spent 23 years surrounded by other Filipinos, yet distancing myself from my ethnic identity. Ironically, it took physically distancing myself from my home state and coming to an HBCU where I am the only Filipino for me to realize my potential and to learn to love myself and my people. Now, I can fight for first-generation and oppressed people, viewing education as the best way for ethnic minorities to achieve individual and collective social mobility. That point explains why I am so passionate about our work in the Office of Diversity and why I have proudly engaged in programs that allow me to celebrate my identity while modeling and encouraging others to do the same. We all should let our identities shine, the same way that the sun and its three stars always shine on the Philippine flag every time it waves in the wind.

Ismail's Reflections.   As a child of parents from Ethiopia and Somalia, I experienced many confusing moments when I could not lean on my parents for explanations for things going on at school in Seattle, because they were learning about the American value system right alongside me. I discovered that being Black was a problem for my White classmates and that being African served as another notch down the social ladder in the eyes of my Black classmates. And when they found out I was Muslim, the teasing and the taunting created self-hate in my heart. After the 9/11 bombings, being Muslim became even more taboo.

When the idea of attending Cedar State was first presented to me, the thought of being 2,000 miles away in the region where slavery and the hanging of Black people were historically commonplace, I was hesitant to attend. However, after remembering the important work of civil rights leaders in that state, I ultimately decided to embrace this new challenge.

Upon my arrival at Cedar State, I realized that neither my culture nor my faith was represented like back home. I understand that having to deal with Muslims on campus is a rarity in the Bible belt, but it can be alienating when prayers are always focused on one religion and pork is often served at university events. Although initially I was lonely, and was unable to use the language or eat traditional foods like *injera*, it eventually became a teaching moment not only for my friends and peers, but also for myself. Being so far from my family and friends, I would help those closest to me learn about my cultural and religious customs. It was exhilarating to walk into a room and have my friends greet me with "*Assalamu alaikum*" ("Peace be unto you") or when I would say thank you in different languages and they knew how to respond. While these were small gestures, they meant a lot to me.

Also, being the only one on campus who could identify as Ethiopian or Somali, I often wore clothes to represent my culture. As a result, I became known on campus as the "Ethiopian/Somali guy" and meaningful questions about my heritage were often asked. I felt fortunate to have friends who genuinely desired to understand me and my culture. Our office modeled the importance of this work (e.g., inclusive prayers), and I noticed that more people on campus became cognizant of the need for this behavior.

Being at Cedar State pushed me to reflect more deeply on my own sense of identity. Even being practically by myself during the holy period of Ramadan as opposed to being surrounded by thousands of Muslims like at home led me to dig deeper into my faith. Having a clearer sense of who I was than I had when I was at home, I realized there were many voids and gaps to my own sense of self; it was wrapped up in either my family's, culture's, or religion's definition of self. While at Cedar State for only two years, what I learned most was to appreciate being fully me. Since returning home for the summer, I discovered that my sense of identity is in partial contrast to my family. And I'm okay with that. I don't feel any less African, any less American, or any less Muslim. I actually feel as though I now embrace all of me plus adding the identity of a Southern gentleman to my own perception of self. When I first left Seattle for Cedar State, a mentor said to me, "It's time to leave the nest and let those wings grow." My wings have definitely grown, and it's a direct result of being away from home, being in the South, and most importantly being at an HBCU that allowed me to grow and find for myself who I truly am.

Discussion

The narratives presented here offer evidence of the importance of context in generating reflection on racial identity. Being at an HBCU for these diverse individuals produced experiences that heightened racial identity salience and enhanced reflective assessment of their racial selves. With regard to Anzaldua's (1987) framework, the narratives connect with the overall sense of relatively healthy management of the borderlands experience.

From Ismail being able to "embrace all of me" to Richard linking his struggle to the larger mission for social justice, the journeys seemed to allow for more profound self-understanding. As both Richard and Ismail suggest, it was precisely being in the minority at an HBCU that necessitated and nurtured the desire to better explore their own ethnic identities. Tony's admission that the questions posed of him led him to ask more questions of himself parallels Derek's discussion of interrogating performances of Whiteness and allyship as a result of the context.

Another critical theme woven throughout these stories is the importance of appreciating the multiplicity of identities that students must maintain and negotiate. From Ismail's acknowledgment of his status as a religious minority to Derek's admission of his double societal privilege as a White male, the writers make reference to matters of intersectionality that may not always be incorporated into campus diversity initiatives and identity conversations. In addition, issues of class, sexuality, and ability status have traditionally been difficult (and often avoided) at HBCUs, and the need for institutions to think more strategically about establishing safe places for particular populations and inclusive space throughout campus stands as a pressing challenge (Baskin-Glover, Johnson, Moses, & Rome, 2014). As HBCUs celebrate the spirit of a shared cultural identity, the notion of highlighting diversity within the Black community offers an exciting and enriching opportunity for students to better understand the contours and unlimited possibilities of identity.

The narratives also advance a richer appreciation of both informal and formal mechanisms in encouraging cross-cultural understanding. Indeed, staff at HBCUs must intentionally construct programs for students to directly learn about diversity, but the more indirect and often unexpected experiences can plausibly be even more critical. For example, the spontaneous and honest late-night conversation between an openly gay student and his heterosexual roommate could plausibly produce greater influence than any speaker or awareness campaign. The testimonials here attest to the centrality of these personal encounters as the impetus for deepening knowledge and commitment to this work. In particular, Ismail makes repeated reference to friendships sparking insight and passion for inclusion.

Supporting this claim, research by Harper and Yeung (2013) suggests that informal campus activities are even more significantly correlated with openness to diverse perspectives than more formal ones. To be clear, formal programs and institutional commitment to fostering diversity are instrumental in establishing a healthy environment that encourages more informal interaction. Thus, as Bowman and Brandenberger (2012) argue, through this dialectic between the formal and informal, positive outcomes in terms of students' attitudes and belief systems can be achieved.

As a result, HBCUs and the individuals whose work centers around cross-cultural understanding may need to be more intentional in generating informal engagement opportunities and support structures that can assist students in navigating through these potentially risky spaces. For example, Nunn et al. (2012) discuss innovative strategies in which HIV information is delivered informally within the African-American community, such as through faith leaders and trained barbers who subtly drop messages encouraging healthy behavior while serving their clients. While it may seem counterintuitive for institutions to plan spontaneous moments of dialogue, individuals can identify ways to invite conversation as well as advance a culture of openness throughout campus. Perhaps social media campaigns building from the principles of social norming can promote a common language for fostering safe and responsible dialogue. As Tony points out, constant questions can inherently represent encounters with "othering," so it is instructive for students to appreciate how to better negotiate conversations to create greater resonance and common ground.

Final Considerations

Lee and Keys (2013) propose that the changing landscape of higher education and shifting enrollment patterns necessitate that HBCUs embrace diversity as a core operating principle. Merely opening doors to diverse students is not sufficient, as creating welcoming and supportive environments will be necessary to retaining them and preparing all members of the campus community for participation in the global marketplace. This chapter addresses the complexity of these efforts, with particular attention to the implications for racial identity work.

Further research in this area is clearly needed. As suggested earlier, of critical importance will be the inclusion of a wider range of identity variables, with stronger emphasis on intersectionality. Researchers must endeavor to capture the divergent aspects of our complex identities and tease out the relative impact of each dimension. Perhaps certain identity variables, or even intersectional combinations, may be more salient and generate greater self-reflection among HBCU students. Additionally, scholarly work to capture the impact of diversity efforts in helping students fashion a healthy sense of self and appreciation of others' identities would be valuable.

Our stories matter. The HBCU story has always celebrated communal strength in the face of hegemony, a resistance and resilience that have produced countless talented graduates who deeply cherish their alma maters.

As the doors swing even wider open to welcome a broader cross-section of students, the stories of this new population must be heard and honored to ensure that schools fully support and benefit from their presence. In turn, these proud institutions will play an integral role in advancing discourse around racial identity development—yet another critical social function that can become part of the HBCU legacy.

References

Anzaldua, G. (1987). *Borderlands/La frontera: The new mestiza*. San Francisco, CA: Aunt Lute Books.

Baskin-Glover, G., Johnson, C., Moses, W., & Rome, K. (2014, September). *Sustaining the future of HBCU through diversity and inclusion*. Panel presentation at the National Historically Black Colleges and Universities Week Conference, Washington, DC.

Blumer, H. G. (1969). *Symbolic interactionism: Perspective and method*. Oakland, CA: University of California Press.

Bowman, N., & Brandenberger, J. (2012). Experiencing the unexpected: Toward a model of college diversity experiences and attitude change. *Review of Higher Education, 35*(2), 179–205.

Closson, R. B., & Henry, W. J. (2008). Racial and ethnic diversity at HBCUs: What can be learned when whites are in the minority? *Multicultural Education, 15*(4), 15–19.

Ellemers, N., Spears, R., & Doosje, B. (2002). Self and social identity. *Annual Review of Psychology, 53*, 161–186.

Ellis, C., Adams, T. E., & Bochner, A. P. (2011). Autoethnography: An overview. *Forum: Qualitative Social Research, 12*(1), 1–18.

Hall, S. (1997). *Representation: Cultural representations and signifying practices*. New York, NY: SAGE Press.

Harper, C., & Yeung, F. (2013). Perceptions of institutional commitment to diversity as a predictor of college students' openness to diverse perspectives. *Review of Higher Education, 37*(1), 25–44.

Lee, J. M., Jr., & Keys, S. W. (2013). *Repositioning HBCUs for the future: Access, success, research, and innovation*. APLU Office of Access and Success Discussion Paper 2013-01. Washington, DC: Association of Public and Land-Grant Universities.

McGuire, W. J., McGuire, C. V., Child, P., & Fujioka, T. (1978). Salience of ethnicity in the spontaneous self-concept as a function of one's ethnic distinctiveness in the social environment. *Journal of Personality and Social Psychology, 36*, 511–520.

McMickens, T. L. (2012). Running the race when race is a factor. *Phi Delta Kappan, 93*(8), 39–43.

Nunn, A., Cornwall, A., Chute, N., Sanders, J., Thomas, G., James, G., . . . Flanigan, T. (2012). Keeping the faith: African American faith leaders' perspectives and recommendations for reducing racial disparities in HIV/AIDS infection. *PLoS ONE, 7*(5), 1–11.

Palmer, R. T., & Maramba, D. C. (in press). A delineation of Asian American and Latino/a students' experiences with faculty at an historically Black college and university. *Journal of College Student Development*.

Peterson, R. D., & Hamrick, F. (2009). White, male, and "minority": Racial consciousness among White male undergraduates attending a historically Black university. *Journal of Higher Education, 80*(1), 34–58.

Stryker, S. (1980). *Symbolic interactionism: A social structural version*. Menlo Park, CA: Benjamin Cummings.

NEW DIRECTIONS FOR HIGHER EDUCATION • DOI: 10.1002/he

Takaki, R. (1998). *Strangers from a different shore: A history of Asian-Americans.* New York, NY: Little, Brown.

Thomas-Lester, A. (2004, October 30). Enrollment is shifting at Black universities. *The Washington Post*, p. C01.

DEREK F. GREENFIELD *is a visionary thought leader, speaker, and consultant dedicated to positive personal and social change. He previously served as director of educational equity and inclusion/Title IX administrator at Alcorn State University in Lorman, Mississippi, and has earned faculty member of the year honors at three different HBCUs.*

TONY INNOUVONG *is a first-generation Lao-American spoken-word artist and community advocate from Seattle, Washington. He obtained his bachelor of science degree at Seattle University and his MBA at Alcorn State University, where he also worked as a research assistant in the Office of the President.*

RICHARD JAY AGLUGUB *is a first-generation college student hailing from the Hawaiian Islands, and is a rising senior psychology major, with future plans to attend graduate school and pursue a career in education.*

ISMAIL A. YUSUF *is an Ethiopian and Somali American from Seattle, Washington. He hopes to pursue a PhD in sociology and eventually teach in higher education.*

NEW DIRECTIONS FOR HIGHER EDUCATION • DOI: 10.1002/he

4

This chapter closely examines trends in White student enrollment at 4-year HBCUs between 1987 and 2012 and discusses the implications of those trends for policy, practice, and future research.

A Closer Examination of White Student Enrollment at HBCUs

C. Rob Shorette II, Andrew T. Arroyo

The ways in which historically Black colleges and universities (HBCUs) experience issues of diversity and inclusion are significantly different from the ways predominantly White institutions (PWIs) experience the same issues. This volume captures some of the unique aspects of the HBCU experience, from the racial identity development of non-Black students of color to the unique needs of lesbian, gay, bisexual, and transgender (LGBT) students at HBCUs. White students enrolled at HBCUs have also been the focus of scholarly research since the later part of the 20th century when they assumed a more prominent role in the HBCU student community. Although the literature is scarce, existing research has examined various aspects of White students' experiences in attending HBCUs, from the historical context of their participation in HBCUs (see, e.g., Gasman, Lundy-Wagner, Ransom, & Bowman, 2010) to the initial stages of choosing to attend an HBCU (see, e.g., Arroyo, Palmer, & Maramba, 2015; Conrad, Brier, & Braxton, 1997) to the social and academic adjustment of White students while attending an HBCU (see, e.g., Arroyo et al., 2015; Strayhorn, 2010).

Moreover, research related to White enrollment in HBCUs has recently emerged. Gasman (2013) detailed the state of racial diversity at HBCUs nationally in her groundbreaking report, *The Changing Face of Historically Black Colleges and Universities*, in which she revealed that White students make up approximately 13% of the total student population at the 105 HBCUs. In Chapter 1 of this volume, Gasman and Nguyen refine the view of White student enrollment by providing a closer examination of 26 HBCUs that had 10% to 88% White students by the year 1980. Our present chapter builds upon their work by further exploring White student enrollment in the specific context of public and private 4-year HBCUs.

NEW DIRECTIONS FOR HIGHER EDUCATION, no. 170, Summer 2015 © 2015 Wiley Periodicals, Inc.
Published online in Wiley Online Library (wileyonlinelibrary.com) • DOI: 10.1002/he.20131

Further Context

Providing a refined perspective on White student enrollments at HBCUs is critical for many reasons. For instance, along with the occasional scholarly report on this issue, national media periodically renews its focus on White student enrollment at HBCUs. A report from *The Journal of Blacks in Higher Education* ("Persisting Myth," 2005) suggests that countless reports and commentaries in the early 2000s were claiming significant surges in White student enrollment at HBCUs, although the data suggested otherwise. Almost a decade after *The Journal of Blacks in Higher Education* released its 2005 report, the thought of White students appropriating HBCUs seems to be persisting. In 2014, for example, *Time* magazine produced an article titled, "Historically Black Colleges Are Becoming More White" (Butrymowicz, 2014), which sparked additional media attention, with many asking the question: How is this supposed surge in White students affecting the HBCU experience?

Considering the impassioned responses the aforementioned reports evoked within the general public and scholarly communities alike, and with *The Journal of Blacks in Higher Education*'s 2005 report in mind, this chapter delves deeper into the data to investigate the validity of these claims made in the media. We sought to establish an updated and refined perspective on White student enrollment at HBCUs by focusing specifically on public and private 4-year institutions. In doing so, we discovered that trends in White student enrollment at 4-year HBCUs lie in direct contradiction to the claims being made in the media. Specifically, White student enrollment at 4-year HBCUs has not increased at all since 1987 and, in fact, has decreased.

Before beginning the analysis, however, we would like to provide two contextual disclaimers for our readers. First, as Lee points out in Chapter 2 of this volume, HBCUs are not monolithic. Essentializing these institutions by presuming homogeneity among them dismisses the unique institutional diversity that comes from differences in geographic location, size, mission, curricular and extracurricular offerings, and so much more. Second, we would like to encourage the reader to take a critical approach to the very topic of White student enrollment and diversity at HBCUs by not applying Eurocentric standards to judge the quality of diversity or assign value to the fact that an HBCU has lower or higher levels of White student enrollment. Not all HBCUs operationalize or prioritize diversity in the same way. HBCUs maintain their historical mission of providing educational opportunities for Black students—opportunities that might not exist without the very existence of HBCUs—and the prevalence of racial inequities in education makes their legacy just as important today as ever before. Therefore, our goal is not to judge and rank HBCUs based on their level of White enrollment, but simply to establish the state of White student enrollment at 4-year HBCUs and discuss potential implications for policy, practice, and future research.

NEW DIRECTIONS FOR HIGHER EDUCATION • DOI: 10.1002/he

Enrollment Trends at 4-Year HBCUs

Due to the economic recession that began in 2008, steadily declining state support of higher education more broadly, and the disproportionately negative effects of the change in Parent PLUS Loan policies on HBCUs, much of the recent public narrative has focused on the challenges HBCUs are facing with undergraduate enrollment (Brown, 2013; Hunter-Gault, 2014; Mullins, 2013). Considering that many HBCUs have been underfunded over time and are relatively tuition-dependent, even the slightest decline in enrollment can have major implications for the operations of these institutions (Hernandez, 2010). As a result, the need to possess a deep understanding of the enrollment behavior of various student populations has become more critical to the financial stability of HBCUs. However, little research has established enrollment trends at HBCUs over the past 15 years. Furthermore, it is important to understand aggregate enrollment trends when discussing the enrollment trends of specific populations.

Aggregate Enrollment Trends at 4-Year HBCUs.   Using the federal definition for HBCUs and drawing from the Delta Cost Project (2010) and the Integrated Postsecondary Education Data System (IPEDS) for the years 1987 to 2012, analysis of 85 four-year public and private institutions is included in this chapter. Of those 85 HBCUs, 45 (53%) are private and 40 (47%) are public, and all of them are concentrated in 19 states, as well as the District of Columbia and the U.S. Virgin Islands. Table 4.1 provides an alphabetical listing of the 4-year HBCUs used for this analysis, including their location, public or private control, and total enrollment as of 2012.

Research has confirmed a declining share of Black students enrolled in HBCUs out of the entire population of Black students attending U.S. higher education institutions. In 1976, Black students at HBCUs made up around 18% of all Blacks in higher education, whereas in 2011 Black HBCU students represented approximately 11% (Gasman, 2013; Redd, 1998). Although these figures speak to a general migration of Black students to non-HBCU institutions, they disguise an important fact that is less discussed: Total enrollment at HBCUs has increased over the same period of time.

Redd (1998) noted that from 1976 to 1998, HBCU enrollment grew from approximately 190,000 to approximately 230,000 students. Aggregate enrollment trends for the 4-year HBCUs included in this study have generally continued along the same path (see Figure 4.1). The increase between 1987 (202,314) and 2012 (271,248) translates to an approximately 34% increase in total enrollment at all 4-year HBCUs. Figures 4.2 and 4.3 show the trends disaggregated by public and private HBCUs, which reveal equally upward trends at rates of approximately 34% each.

White Student Enrollment at All 4-Year HBCUs.   Racial diversity has been evolving on the campuses of HBCUs. In a recently released report, Gasman notes that the share of White enrollment at all HBCUs has generally hovered around 10% to 13% over the past 20 years (Gasman, 2013).

NEW DIRECTIONS FOR HIGHER EDUCATION • DOI: 10.1002/he

Table 4.1. Four-Year HBCUs (Location, Institutional Control, and Total Enrollment)

Name of Institution	State	Control	Total Enrollment in 2012
Alabama A&M University	AL	Public	4,853
Alabama State University	AL	Public	5,816
Albany State University	GA	Public	4,275
Alcorn State University	MS	Public	3,950
Allen University	SC	Private	672
Arkansas Baptist College	AR	Private	1,082
Benedict College	SC	Private	2,917
Bennett College for Women	NC	Private	707
Bethune-Cookman University	FL	Private	3,543
Bluefield State College	WV	Public	1,935
Bowie State University	MD	Public	5,421
Central State University	OH	Public	2,152
Cheyney University of Pennsylvania	PA	Public	1,284
Claflin University	SC	Private	1,946
Clark Atlanta University	GA	Private	3,419
Concordia College–Selma	AL	Private	611
Coppin State University	MD	Public	3,612
Delaware State University	DE	Public	4,324
Dillard University	LA	Private	1,307
Edward Waters College	FL	Private	925
Elizabeth City State University	NC	Public	2,878
Fayetteville State University	NC	Public	6,060
Fisk University	TN	Private	620
Florida A&M University	FL	Public	12,057
Florida Memorial University	FL	Private	1,579
Fort Valley State University	GA	Public	3,568
Grambling State University	LA	Public	5,277
Hampton University	VA	Private	4,765
Harris-Stowe State University	MO	Public	1,484
Howard University	DC	Private	10,002
Huston-Tillotson University	TX	Private	918
Interdenominational Theological Center	GA	Private	827
Jackson State University	MS	Public	8,819
Jarvis Christian College	TX	Private	603
Johnson C. Smith University	NC	Private	1,669
Kentucky State University	KY	Public	2,524
Lane College	TN	Private	1,512
Langston University	OK	Public	2,518
Le Moyne–Owen College	TN	Private	1,078
Lincoln University	MO	Public	3,205
Lincoln University of Pennsylvania	PA	Public	2,101
Livingstone College	NC	Private	1,111
Miles College	AL	Private	1,691

(Continued)

Table 4.1. Continued

Name of Institution	State	Control	Total Enrollment in 2012
Mississippi Valley State University	MS	Public	2,479
Morehouse College	GA	Private	2,374
Morgan State University	MD	Public	7,952
Morris College	SC	Private	874
Norfolk State University	VA	Public	7,100
North Carolina A&T State University	NC	Public	10,636
North Carolina Central University	NC	Public	8,604
Oakwood University	AL	Private	2,019
Paine College	GA	Private	837
Paul Quinn College	TX	Private	192
Philander Smith College	AR	Private	666
Prairie View A&M University	TX	Public	8,336
Rust College	MS	Private	934
Saint Augustine's College	NC	Private	1,442
Saint Paul's College	VA	Private	112
Savannah State University	GA	Public	4,582
Shaw University	NC	Private	2,183
South Carolina State University	SC	Public	3,807
Southern University and A&M College	LA	Public	6,397
Southern University at New Orleans	LA	Public	2,820
Southwestern Christian College	TX	Private	206
Spelman College	GA	Private	2,145
Stillman College	AL	Private	1,019
Talladega College	AL	Private	1,203
Tennessee State University	TN	Public	8,740
Texas College	TX	Private	845
Texas Southern University	TX	Public	9,646
Tougaloo College	MS	Private	972
Tuskegee University	AL	Private	3,117
University of Arkansas at Pine Bluff	AR	Public	2,828
University of Maryland Eastern Shore	MD	Public	4,454
University of the District of Columbia	DC	Public	5,110
University of the Virgin Islands	VI	Public	2,423
Virginia State University	VA	Public	6,208
Virginia Union University	VA	Private	1,751
Virginia University of Lynchburg	VA	Private	540
Voorhees College	SC	Private	648
West Virginia State University	WV	Public	2,644
Wilberforce University	OH	Private	518
Wiley College	TX	Private	1,401
Winston-Salem State University	NC	Public	5,689
Xavier University of Louisiana	LA	Private	3,178
Total Enrollment			**271,248**

Source: U.S. Department of Education, National Center for Education Statistics, Integrated Postsecondary Education Data System (IPEDS), Fall 2012.

Figure 4.1. Total Enrollment at All 4-Year HBCUs, 1987–2012

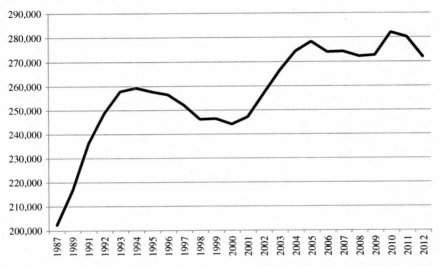

Source: U.S. Department of Education, National Center for Education Statistics, Integrated Postsecondary Education Data System (IPEDS).

Figure 4.2. Total Enrollment at Public 4-Year HBCUs, 1987–2012

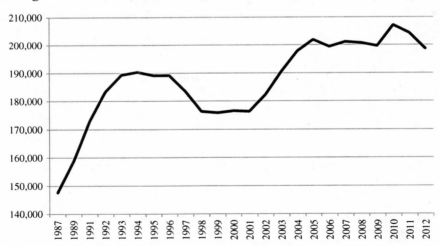

Source: U.S. Department of Education, National Center for Education Statistics, Integrated Postsecondary Education Data System (IPEDS).

Figure 4.3. Total Enrollment at Private 4-Year HBCUs, 1987–2012

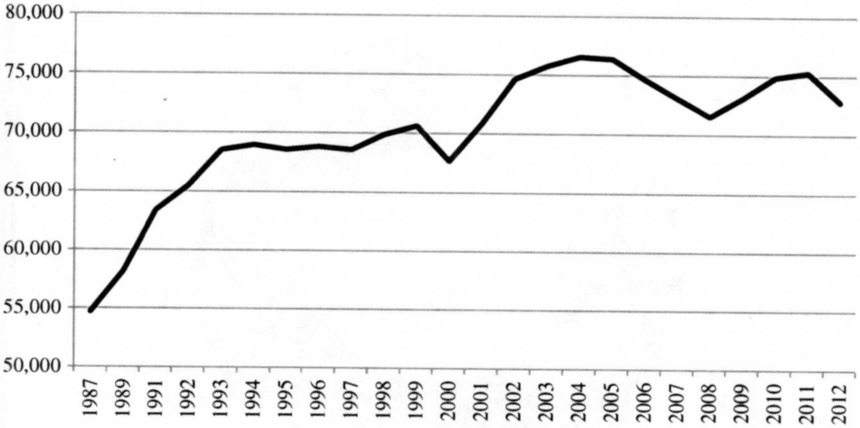

Source: U.S. Department of Education, National Center for Education Statistics, Integrated Postsecondary Education Data System (IPEDS).

This finding is important for countering arguments that HBCUs perpetuate segregation. However, when excluding 2-year institutions and graduate medical schools such as Morehouse School of Medicine and Meharry Medical College, data for 4-year HBCUs reveal lower White participation. Black enrollments make up more than 80% of total enrollment and White enrollments make up 7%, with the next largest category being "Race/ethnicity unknown" at almost 4% (see Figure 4.4).

After hitting a peak in total White enrollment in the early 1990s at over 32,000, White enrollment has steadily decreased in both total number and mean share of total enrollment. From 1987 to 2012, not only have 4-year HBCUs experienced a decline in White enrollment of more than 9,000 students (or approximately –30%; see Figure 4.5), but White students also constitute a significantly smaller share of total enrollment, as they have gone from more than 14% to less than 8% (see Figure 4.6).

White Student Enrollment at 4-Year HBCUs, Public Versus Private. As far as total numbers are concerned, public HBCUs experienced the largest decline in White student enrollment between 1987 and 2012. White student enrollment at the 40 public HBCUs was higher than 30,000 during the early 1990s, but experienced a nearly 40% decline and recently hit an all-time low during 2011 and 2012 at approximately 19,000 White students (see Figure 4.7).

The combination of an increase in total enrollment and a decline in White student enrollment at public HBCUs produced a significant decrease in the share of White student enrollment as well. In 1987 the share of White enrollment was around 18%; in 2010 it was just under 10%.

Figure 4.4. Percentage of Enrollment by Race at All 4-Year HBCUs in 2012

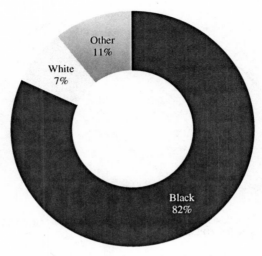

Source: U.S. Department of Education, National Center for Education Statistics, Integrated Postsecondary Education Data System (IPEDS).

White student enrollment at private HBCUs, in contrast, remained relatively stagnant after a steep decline in the late 1980s. Although public HBCUs experienced more variation in both total enrollment and White student enrollment, private HBCUs did experience declines in the share of White student enrollment due to the increase in total student

Figure 4.5. Total White Enrollment at All 4-Year HBCUs, 1987–2012

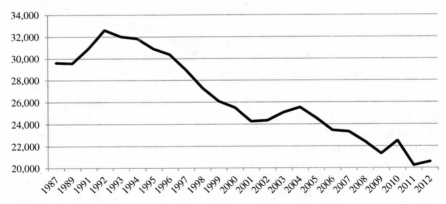

Source: U.S. Department of Education, National Center for Education Statistics, Integrated Postsecondary Education Data System (IPEDS).

Figure 4.6. Percentage of White Enrollment at All 4-Year HBCUs, 1987–2012

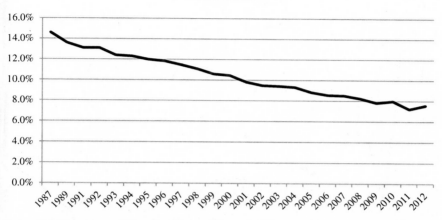

Source: U.S. Department of Education, National Center for Education Statistics, Integrated Postsecondary Education Data System (IPEDS).

enrollment. While total student enrollment in private HBCUs increased from almost 54,700 in 1987 to nearly 73,000 in 2012, White student enrollment at private HBCUs during the period from 1993 on generally hovered around 1,500 (see Figure 4.8). The increase in total enrollment, however, had less of an effect on the percentage of White students at private HBCUs

Figure 4.7. Total White Enrollment at Public 4-Year HBCUs, 1987–2012

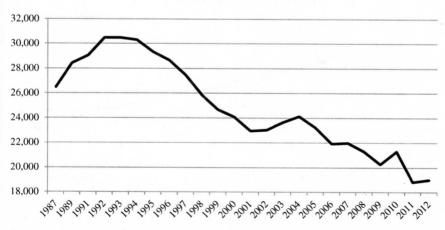

Source: U.S. Department of Education, National Center for Education Statistics, Integrated Postsecondary Education Data System (IPEDS).

New Directions for Higher Education • DOI: 10.1002/he

Figure 4.8. Total White Enrollment at Private 4-Year HBCUs, 1987–2012

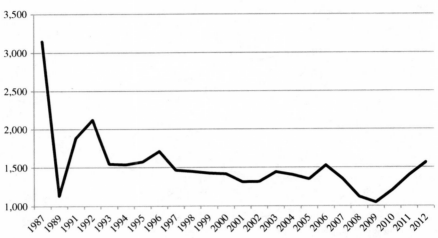

Source: U.S. Department of Education, National Center for Education Statistics, Integrated Postsecondary Education Data System (IPEDS).

than at public HBCUs, with the share of White student enrollment at private HBCUs (excluding 1987) ranging from a high of 3% in 1991 to a low of 1.4 percent in 2009 (see Figure 4.9).

White Enrollment at 2-Year HBCUs.   Although the focus of this chapter is on 4-year HBCUs, it is useful to provide some context for 2-year

Figure 4.9. Percentage of White Enrollment at 4-Year HBCUs, 1987–2012, Public Versus Private

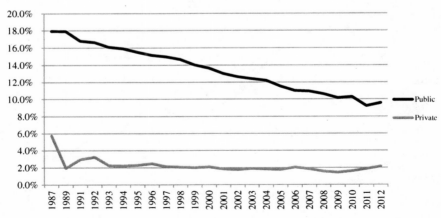

Source: U.S. Department of Education, National Center for Education Statistics, Integrated Postsecondary Education Data System (IPEDS).

NEW DIRECTIONS FOR HIGHER EDUCATION • DOI: 10.1002/he

Table 4.2. Total Enrollment and White Enrollment at 2-Year HBCUs in 2012

Two-Year Institutions	Total Enrollment in 2012	White Enrollment in 2012	Share of White Enrollment
Bishop State Community College	3,791	1,122	29.6%
Clinton College	139	0	0%
Coahoma Community College	2,305	58	2.5%
Denmark Technical College	2,003	70	3.5%
Gadsden State Community College	5,882	4,058	69%
H. Councill Trenholm State Technical College	1,445	523	36.2%
J. F. Drake State Technical College	1,248	525	42.1%
Lawson State Community College	3,419	493	14.4%
St. Philip's College	10,313	3,133	30.4%
Shelton State Community College	5,104	2,759	54.1%
Shorter College	52	0	0%
Southern University at Shreveport	2,937	335	11.4%
Totals for 2-Year HBCUs	**38,638**	**13,076**	**34%**
Totals for 4-Year HBCUs	**271,248**	**19,009**	**7%**

Source: U.S. Department of Education, National Center for Education Statistics, Integrated Postsecondary Education Data System (IPEDS).

HBCUs in order to better understand the big picture of White enrollment at all HBCUs. As has been demonstrated in the previous sections, White enrollment at 4-year HBCUs has declined over the past two decades. Just as important to understand, however, is how 2-year institutions are influencing the statistics for White enrollment at all HBCUs. Of the 100 total HBCUs, the dozen 2-year HBCUs enroll nearly 39,000 students—13,000 (approximately 34%) of whom are White (see Table 4.2). Despite their relatively small representation among all HBCUs, 2-year historically Black colleges disproportionately enroll 41% of White students at all HBCUs, as shown in the table. As a result, viewing White enrollment in the aggregate disguises the fact that the demographic makeup of 2-year HBCUs is significantly different from that of 4-year HBCUs.

Implications of White Enrollment Trends

In this chapter, we have offered an updated and refined perspective on White student enrollment at 4-year public and private HBCUs. Despite some media fanfare suggesting widespread surges in White enrollment at HBCUs over recent years, the data reveal a different picture. Blacks comprise the overwhelming majority of HBCU enrollments at all but a handful of HBCUs (Gasman, 2013; Lee, 2012), and White participation in 4-year

NEW DIRECTIONS FOR HIGHER EDUCATION • DOI: 10.1002/he

HBCUs has declined since the 1990s. Here we offer implications of this downward adjustment for research, policy, and practice.

Implications for Research.   Due to HBCUs' historical and contemporary significance for Black students, most HBCU-based research focuses on Blacks. For example, Arroyo and Gasman's (2014) synthesis of the HBCU-based literature for Black college student success offers a representative picture of the large number of these studies. Research on White and other non-Black HBCU students occupies a smaller place in the literature (see, e.g., Arroyo et al., 2015; Brown, 2002; Carter & Fountaine, 2012; Closson & Henry, 2008a, 2008b; Conrad et al., 1997; Dwyer, 2006; Gendrin & Chandler, 2011; Hall & Closson, 2005; Nixon & Henry, 1991; Palmer, Arroyo, & Maramba, 2014; Palmer & Maramba, in press-a, in press-b; Peterson & Hamrick, 2009; Strayhorn, 2010). However, to our knowledge, no existing study on White HBCU students has contextualized its findings within the complicated White enrollment picture presented in this chapter.

Several implications for research follow from these findings. First, scholars should create a more robust and applicable literature on White students by carefully contextualizing future studies. In part, this means describing specific White population trends for the general type of institution a researcher is studying (e.g., 4- or 2-year, public or private), rather than presenting White enrollments in the aggregate. Equally, it means providing greater detail regarding the specific White enrollment trends at the given institution(s) under study. Knowing whether a given institution has experienced steady, declining, or increasing White enrollments over the years leading up to the study—as well as the percentages of those enrollments—can help other researchers and practitioners assess and apply the findings appropriately.

Additionally, we suggest reinterpreting the existing research literature on White students' experiences at HBCUs through the lens of the data presented in this chapter. According to our evaluation of the literature, the sites for every study on White experiences at HBCUs have been 4-year institutions. None have utilized 2-year institutions. However, despite this consistent 4-year focus, each of these studies contextualizes itself within White population trends using one or more of the following data sources: (a) aggregate 2-year and 4-year figures (see, e.g., Arroyo et al., 2015; Hall & Closson, 2005; Peterson & Hamrick, 2009); (b) outdated figures that predate declines in White enrollment (see, e.g., Brown, 2002; Dwyer, 2006); or (c) examples of White growth that refer to sensationalized popular press stories and/or outliers such as Bluefield State College in West Virginia (see, e.g., Carter & Fountaine, 2012). Some studies leave out White population trends completely (see, e.g., Closson & Henry, 2008a, 2008b; Strayhorn, 2010). Although the ways in which these data sources were used in the aforementioned research do not invalidate their findings, wrong, misused, or missing trend data can inhibit the reader's understanding of their relative meaning and significance.

For a closer look at how these issues manifest in the literature, we turn to the example of Carter and Fountaine's (2012) exploration of engagement factors of White HBCU students. To be clear, our goal in selecting this study is to offer a representative example of what is typical in the literature on White HBCU students in a collegial context, and not to criticize this particular study. The authors conducted individual interviews and focus groups with White students at two HBCUs that they described as comprehensive, regional, and public (i.e., 4-year). Although the findings are presented in a clear and compelling fashion, significant contextual problems impede full understanding.

To begin, Carter and Fountaine (2012) provide no racial/ethnic demographic information for the two sites, leaving a reader with critical questions: Did Whites comprise similar percentages at each institution? What were the percentages? This oversight limits researchers' ability to replicate the study, create comparisons and contrasts with other studies, and hypothesize whether the results would have been different in an HBCU with greater or lesser numbers of White students relative to Black students. Even more concerning (in our view) is that Carter and Fountaine situated their study under the claim of "a recent influx of White students" (p. 53) at HBCUs broadly. A close examination of their citations in support of this claim reveals a reliance on misinterpreted sources, popular press sources, and derivative sources rather than current primary source figures.

Further, they assert that "many [HBCUs] have larger White undergraduate enrollments than Black undergraduate enrollments" (Carter & Fountaine, 2012, p. 49), which requires a generous interpretation of the word *many* in light of the facts presented in this volume and even in their own narrative. Although we concur with the authors that there is a need "to better understand White students' collegiate experiences at HBCUs" (p. 50) and we appreciate their acknowledgment of the diversity of White students "who possessed multiple identities and assumed various roles in their personal lives" (p. 57), we suggest that connecting the impetus for studying White HBCU students to any sort of widespread influx is a mistake with important consequences. And to reiterate, our purpose in selecting Carter and Fountaine's study is not to impugn them. Indeed, similar issues are pervasive in this subfield of HBCU research. But we would argue that future research must do a better job of contextualizing studies to ameliorate these issues, improve the quality of the studies, and facilitate more useful findings.

In addition to providing richer descriptions of the context in which future studies are situated, researchers should consider focusing attention on the experiences of students at 2-year HBCUs. Since existing literature focuses exclusively on the experiences of White students at 4-year HBCUs, no known research captures the experiences of White students at 2-year HBCUs. As a result, unanswered questions abound, such as: What is the college-choice process for White students at 2-year HBCUs? How many White students at 2-year HBCUs go on to 4-year HBCUs as opposed to 4-year PWIs? Do the experiences of White students at 2-year HBCUs differ from 4-year HBCU students? Investigating these issues further and studying the experiences of White students at 2-year institutions will deepen our understanding of diversity at HBCUs in general and provide critical context through which researchers should view issues affecting White HBCU students in the future.

Implications for Policy and Practice.   Quite possibly the most important question that emerges after viewing the data in this chapter is this: Why has White student enrollment at public 4-year HBCUs been steadily declining over the past two decades? Considering that enrollment management is a high priority for higher education institutions in tight economic conditions, understanding how HBCUs factor into the college-choice process for various demographic groups and why White students seem to be choosing HBCUs less and less over time is essential. Because the answers to these questions have broad implications for the HBCU community, they should be addressed collectively by researchers, practitioners, and policy makers alike.

Policy makers at 4-year HBCUs can use this decline in White enrollment as an opportunity to engage in strategic conversations relative to their historical missions. As we stated earlier in this chapter, HBCUs should avoid participating in a Eurocentric value system that prizes White students over others. In some cases—and perhaps many cases—policy makers at HBCUs might consider their work with predominantly Black populations unfinished and in need of prioritized attention. Becoming concerned with White enrollments might lead to confused policies that ultimately divert resources from where they are needed most. At the same time, for HBCUs that do seek greater racial diversity, strategic discussions around enrollment management must be founded in accurate data that are specific to institutional context as opposed to potentially misleading and unrepresentative aggregate data.

Other practical implications include potentially overestimating the participation and representation of White students at HBCUs. This is important because a student who is part of a 2% minority may face greater race-based pressures than a student belonging to a 40% minority. Practitioners at 4-year HBCUs should be sensitive to the actual numbers of White students on campus, including the upward or downward trends in that population, when considering how to serve them best. In other words, practitioners should not assume anything when making decisions, but should allow numbers and research related to specific institutional contexts to drive decisions. Similarly, policy makers at the federal and state level must also consider HBCUs in their proper context, especially in light of the fact that public 4-year HBCUs might face different pressures to reverse White enrollment declines than private HBCUs due to the legal rulings previously cited.

Conclusion

After taking a closer look at White enrollment at HBCUs, two points become clear: (1) institutional context matters because the demographic makeup of 2-year and 4-year, and public and private HBCUs are very different; and (2) White enrollment at 4-year HBCUs has steadily declined over the past two decades. In response to these revelations, researchers, practitioners, and policy makers should take a more critical and nuanced approach to viewing the issue of White student enrollment at HBCUs. Because of the fact that there is an observable decline in White enrollment and our knowledge of the experiences of White students at HBCUs is still relatively limited, work remains to support the success of all students and ultimately strengthen the overall HBCU community.

References

Arroyo, A. T., & Gasman, M. (2014). An HBCU-based approach for Black college student success: With implications for all institutions. *American Journal of Education, 121*(1), 57–85.

Arroyo, A. T., Palmer, R. T., & Maramba, D. C. (2015, April). *Is it a different world? Providing a holistic understanding of the experiences and perceptions of non-Black students of historically Black colleges and universities.* Paper presented at the American Educational Research Association Conference, Chicago, IL.

Brown, M. C. (2002). Good intentions: Collegiate desegregation and transdemographic enrollments. *Review of Higher Education, 25*(3), 263–280.

Brown, S. (2013, September 13). Historically Black N.C. schools battle declining enrollment, look to move forward. *The Daily Tar Heel.* Retrieved from http://www.daily tarheel.com/article/2013/09/hbcus-0919

Butrymowicz, S. (2014, June 27). Historically Black colleges are becoming more White. *Time.* Retrieved from http://time.com/2907332/historically-black-colleges -increasingly-serve-white-students/

Carter, J. D., & Fountaine, T. (2012). An analysis of White student engagement at public HBCUs. *Journal of Educational Foundations at Stockton College, 26*(3–4), 49–66.

Closson, R. B., & Henry, W. J. (2008a). Racial and ethnic diversity at HBCUs: What can be learned when Whites are in the minority? *Multicultural Education, 15*(4), 15–19.

Closson, R. B., & Henry, W. J. (2008b). The social adjustment of undergraduate White students in the minority on an historically Black college campus. *Journal of College Student Development, 49*(6), 517–534.

Conrad, C. F., Brier, E. M., & Braxton, J. M. (1997). Factors contributing to the matriculation of White students in public HBCUs. *Journal of a Just and Caring Education, 3*(1), 37–62.

Delta Cost Project. (2010). *IPEDS Analytics: Delta Cost Project Database.* Retrieved from http://nces.ed.gov/ipeds/deltacostproject/

Dwyer, B. (2006). Framing the effect of multiculturalism on diversity outcomes among students at historically Black colleges and universities. *Educational Foundations, 20*(1, 2), 37–59.

Gasman, M. (2013). *The changing face of historically Black colleges and universities.* Philadelphia, PA: Center for Minority Serving Institutions, University of Pennsylvania.

Gasman, M., Lundy-Wagner, V., Ransom, T., & Bowman, N., III. (2010). *Unearthing promise and potential: Our nation's historically Black colleges and universities.* San Francisco, CA: Jossey-Bass.

Gendrin, D. M., & Chandler, K. (2011). Interethnic encounters between African American and Vietnamese American students in the HBCU context. *Human Communication,* 15(2), 103–119.

Hall, B., & Closson, R. B. (2005). When the majority is in the minority: White graduate students' social adjustment at a historically Black university. *Journal of College Student Development,* 46(1), 28–42.

Hernandez, A. (2010). Independent thinking: HBCUs explore ways to liberate themselves from tuition dependence. *Diverse Issues in Higher Education,* 27(5), 12.

Hunter-Gault, C. (2014, February 9). Hard times at Howard U. *The New York Times.* Retrieved from http://www.nytimes.com/2014/02/09/education/edlife/a-historically -black-college-is-rocked-by-the-economy-infighting-and-a-changing-demographic .html

Lee, J. M., Jr. (2012). An examination of the participation of African American students in graduate education without public HBCUs. In R. T. Palmer, A. Hilton, & T. Fountaine (Eds.), *Black graduate education at Historically Black Colleges and Universities* (pp. 61–82). Charlotte, NC: Information Age.

Mullins, D. (2013, October 22). Historically Black colleges in financial fight for their future. *Al Jazeera America.* Retrieved from http://america.aljazeera.com/articles/2013/ 10/22/historically-blackcollegesfightfortheirfuture.html

Nixon, H. L., & Henry, W. J. (1991). White students at the Black university: Their experiences regarding acts of racial intolerance. *Equity & Excellence in Education,* 25(2–4), 121–123.

Palmer, R. T., Arroyo, A. T., & Maramba, D. C. (2014, November). *Exploring the perceptions of HBCU student affairs professionals toward the diversification of HBCUs.* Paper presented at the Association for the Study of Higher Education Conference, Washington, DC.

Palmer, R. T., & Maramba, D. C. (in press-a). A delineation of Asian American and Latino/a students' experiences with faculty at an historically Black college and university. *Journal of College Student Development.*

Palmer, R. T., & Maramba, D. C. (in press-b). Racial microaggressions among Asian American and Latino/a students at an HBCU. *Journal of College Student Development.*

The persisting myth that the Black colleges are becoming Whiter. (2005). News & Views. *The Journal of Blacks in Higher Education.* Retrieved from http://www.jbhe.com/ news_views/47_myth_blackcolleges.html

Peterson, R. D., & Hamrick, F. A. (2009). White, male, and "minority": Racial consciousness among white male undergraduates attending a historically Black university. *Journal of Higher Education,* 80(1), 34–58.

Redd, K. E. (1998). Historically Black colleges and universities: Making a comeback. In J. P. Merisotis & C. T. O'Brien (Eds.), *New Directions for Higher Education: No. 102. Minority-serving institutions: Distinct purposes, common goals* (pp. 33–43). San Francisco, CA: Jossey-Bass.

Strayhorn, T. (2010). Majority as temporary minority: Examining the influence of faculty-student relationships on satisfaction among white undergraduates at historically black colleges and universities. *Journal of College Student Development,* 51(5), 509–524.

NEW DIRECTIONS FOR HIGHER EDUCATION • DOI: 10.1002/he

C. Rob Shorette II recently earned a PhD in higher education from Michigan State University. Dr. Shorette is an educator and researcher focused on diversity and equity in higher education, a former HBCU presidential aide, and an HBCU alumnus.

Andrew T. Arroyo is an assistant professor of interdisciplinary studies and living-learning communities faculty liaison at Norfolk State University, a public HBCU. He is also an affiliate with the Center for Minority Serving Institutions, University of Pennsylvania.

5

Drawing from a larger study on Asian Americans and Latino/as at HBCUs, this chapter focuses exclusively on the Latino/a students, sheds light on factors that motivated Latino/a students to attend a historically Black university, and discusses the on-campus experiences of these students. The chapter provides insight into what HBCUs might do to help increase a sense of belonging among Latino/a students.

From Matriculation to Engagement on Campus: Delineating the Experiences of Latino/a Students at a Public Historically Black University

Robert T. Palmer, Dina C. Maramba, Taryn Ozuna Allen, Ramon B. Goings

Historically Black colleges and universities (HBCUs) emerged during a period when predominantly White institutions (PWIs), primarily in the Southern states, excluded Blacks from participating in postsecondary education (Gasman, Lundy-Wagner, Ransom, & Bowman, 2010). Although HBCUs were created to provide an educational opportunity for Blacks, these institutions have never prohibited students, faculty, and staff from other racial and ethnic backgrounds from matriculating into and working there. As Marybeth Gasman and Thai-Huy Nguyen explained in Chapter 1, HBCUs have always been welcoming to diverse populations. However, since their founding, HBCUs have enrolled a predominantly Black student population. For example, in *The Changing Face of Historically Black Colleges and Universities*, a report that Gasman (2013) wrote for the Center for Minority Serving Institutions at the University of Pennsylvania, she noted that in 1950 Black students made up almost 100% of the student enrollment of HBCUs. By 1980, however, Black students represented 80% of the HBCU student enrollment.

Today, Black students constitute 76% of students attending HBCUs while students from other racial and ethnic groups make up the remaining 24%. Within that 24% of non-Black students, 13% are White, 5% are students whose race or ethnicity is unknown, 3% are Latino/a, 1%

NEW DIRECTIONS FOR HIGHER EDUCATION, no. 170, Summer 2015   © 2015 Wiley Periodicals, Inc.
Published online in Wiley Online Library (wileyonlinelibrary.com) • DOI: 10.1002/he.20132

Table 5.1. HBCUs With High Enrollments of Latino/a Students by Percentage

HBCU	Percentage of Latino/a Students
St. Phillip's College	53.12%
Huston-Tillotson College	18.44%
Paul Quinn College	10.94%
Texas College	9.23%
Jarvis Christian College	7.46%
University of District of Columbia	6.96%
Prairie View A&M University	6.24%
Fayetteville State University	5.86%
University of Virgin Islands–U.S. Virgin Islands	5.76%
Wiley College	5.47%

Note: Adapted from "10 Historically Black Colleges and Universities with the Highest Latino/a Population," Center for Minority Serving Institutions, University of Pennsylvania. Retrieved from http://msilineup.com/2014/10/12/10-historically-black-colleges-and-universities-with-the-highest -latinoa-population/

are Asian-American, 1% identify as two or more races, and 1% are classified as nonresident aliens (Gasman, 2013). Some 4-year HBCUs, such as Lincoln University of Missouri, West Virginia State University, and Bluefield State College, now have a majority enrollment of White students. Additionally, St. Philip's College, a 2-year historically Black college in San Antonio, Texas, has a majority enrollment of Latino/a students and is also recognized as a Hispanic-serving institution (St. Philip's College, 2014). There are also nine 4-year HBCUs with large enrollments of Latino/a students, according to recent data from the Center for Minority Serving Institutions. Table 5.1 provides a list of those institutions with the percentages of Latino/a students enrolled.

Since 2000, HBCUs have increased their enrollment of Latino/as by 90% (Lee, 2012). Palmer and Maramba (in press-a, in press-b) predict that the enrollment of non-Black students (e.g., Asian-American, Latino/a, and White) attending HBCUs will continue for several reasons. First, legal cases such as *Adams v. Richardson* (1972) and *United States v. Fordice* (1992) mandate that HBCUs increase their racial diversification. Second, as Black students, who traditionally relied on HBCUs to access postsecondary education, seek other venues, such as PWIs and for-profit institutions (Palmer & Wood, 2012; Patton, 2012), HBCUs are being more intentional about recruiting non-Black students. Some HBCU leaders as well as scholars have argued that if HBCUs are going to remain economically healthy, it is vital that they be more strategic in recruiting and retaining non-Black students (Gasman, 2009; Lee, 2013). To help HBCUs achieve these objectives, this chapter provides a summary of findings from a large study on Asian Americans and Latino/as at a historically Black university. For more details about the methodology, data analysis, trustworthiness, limitations,

New Directions for Higher Education • DOI: 10.1002/he

and findings of the study, see Palmer and Maramba (in press-a, in press-b). Two questions guided this study:

1. What factors influence Asian Americans and Latino/a students' decision to matriculate into an HBCU?
2. What are the on-campus experiences of Asian Americans and Latino/as at HBCUs?

While the study focused on Asian Americans and Latino/as, this chapter focuses specifically on the Latino/a students included in this study and is divided into three parts. The first part discusses factors that motivated Latino/as to attend this historically Black university. Second, the chapter discusses the on-campus experiences of Latino/as at this university. Third is a discussion of what all HBCUs should do to help increase the sense of belonging among this student demographic. The chapter concludes with a consideration of the implications for future research.

Factors Encouraging Latino/a Students to Attend a Public HBCU

Despite the fact that all study participants attended a particular HBCU as undergraduates, some of them had no prior familiarity with HBCUs. In fact, two of the Latina participants recalled that they had never heard of HBCUs. They explained that they played on a softball team in high school and were given an athletic scholarship to attend this HBCU. However, the two participants expressed that the coach who recruited them to the school never explained that it was an HBCU. The participants did not discover that the school was an HBCU until they arrived on campus and noticed that most of the students were Black. Of course, this experience was not reflective of all the Latino/a students. Some participants heard about HBCUs from friends and decided to do more research on these institutions, which resulted in their application to and attendance at the HBCU. For example, one participant, a Latino, remembers driving in a car with his girlfriend and seeing a paper or advertisement with the acronym HBCU. He asked his girlfriend, "What are HBCUs?" She explained that they are institutions that provide educational access to disadvantaged students. Her definition, albeit laconic, provided the impetus for him to want to learn more. Subsequently, he did more research on HBCUs and was intrigued by the opportunity to attend.

Though the participants' knowledge about HBCUs varied, they were all inspired to attend this university because it offered a particular major of interest, such as social work, education, or engineering. For example, one Latina participant wanted to be a social worker and desired to work specifically with inner-city populations. Therefore, she thought that attending an HBCU would best position and prepare her for future professional aspirations. Several Latino participants were motivated to attend this university

NEW DIRECTIONS FOR HIGHER EDUCATION • DOI: 10.1002/he

because it had a reputable engineering program. They believed that this program would provide them with a quality education and help them get high-paying jobs upon graduation.

While participants were encouraged to attend a public HBCU because of the school's low tuition and proximity to their homes, they all discussed how the school's diversity scholarship served as an additional factor that motivated them to attend. For example, a Latina participant explained that she was initially weighing offers from several other universities. However, when she found out that she was going to receive the diversity scholarship from this public historically Black university she became more interested in it.

Interestingly, the factors that attracted the Latino/a participants to this university are similar to the ones that have encouraged White students to attend HBCUs. For example, in a multisite case study conducted to understand factors that contributed to the matriculation of White students into public HBCUs, Conrad, Brier, and Braxton (1997) found that these students were motivated to attend HBCUs for at least three reasons. First, HBCUs offered quality and reputable majors in fields in high demand, such as education, nursing, and engineering. Second was HBCUs' lower tuition; in fact, the tuition of public HBCUs is typically lower than private HBCUs or their public or private PWI counterparts (Palmer, Davis, & Maramba, 2011). Third was the close proximity of HBCUs to the White students' homes.

The Latino/a participants cited the diversity scholarship as one of the aspects that factored into their decision to attend an HBCU. Public HBCUs are not the only HBCUs offering this type of financial incentive to attract non-Black students to campus. Howard University, a private HBCU in Washington, DC, offers similar types of scholarships to non-Black students (Paddock, 2013). While these diversity scholarships are available, it is not clear how much money non-Black students receive from them, nor is it clear if the money is coming from the HBCUs themselves or from another entity. It is also not clear whether the funding for these scholarships is based on limited or unlimited financial resources. The one aspect that is clear, however, is that the diversity scholarship has played an important role in helping HBCUs attract non-Black students, such as Latino/as.

On-Campus Experiences of Latino/a Students

After the participants matriculated into this historically Black university, they experienced several challenges. One of the first challenges involved the institution's faculty. While all participants praised the faculty for being supportive and accessible out of class, they complained that faculty members were culturally exclusive in the classroom. Specifically, they stated that the faculty focused too much on Black issues and concerns and seemed to lack knowledge about other cultures. They also noticed that when faculty discussed issues related to Latino/as, they expected the Latino/a students in the classroom to be the spokespersons for all Latino/as. Participants felt that these experiences engendered a chilly climate in the classroom. All participants stated that HBCU faculty not only needed to be more informed about other cultures, but also needed to demonstrate that knowledge while teaching in order to create a more inclusive and educationally rich learning environment for all students in the classroom—Black and non-Black.

Participants also noted that they experienced other incidents that added to the chilly academic climate at this HBCU. As researchers, we characterized these experiences as racial microaggressions. Racial microaggressions are subtle forms of racism that can engender psychological stress and impede task performance (Sue et al., 2007). In the context of higher education, racial microaggressions can make students who already feel they are at the margins of the institution feel even more isolated, and can hinder their academic performance. Sue et al. (2007) identified three variations of racial microaggressions: (1) microassault, (2) microinsults, (3) and microinvalidations. A microassault is the same as blatant racism and includes using derogatory language and behavior to attack someone based on his or her overt or perceived racial differences. Microinsults are exchanges that denote insensitivity or disregard for that person's race or identity. Finally, microinvalidations are experiences or interactions that "exclude, negate, or nullify the psychological thoughts, feelings, or experiential reality of a person of color" (p. 274). A microinvalidation happens when, for example, a minority person shares with a White colleague the experience of racial microaggressions at work, and the response from the White colleague is that the minority colleague is being hypersensitive.

Participants in this study experienced two forms of racial microaggressions: microassaults and microinsults (Sue et al., 2007). Several Latinas explained that when they initially arrived on the university campus, they endured unpleasant stares by their Black peers, which caused them to feel uncomfortable and unwelcome on campus. Some of their Black peers even accused them of being at the wrong institution. Despite these examples of microassault, these participants explained that as their Black peers became used to seeing them on campus, the unpleasant stares and comments stopped.

One participant shared the experience of a microassault when she encountered an older Black woman walking with her daughter on campus. When the woman saw the participant and her friends, she stopped, pointed at the Latina women, and said, "You wouldn't have seen that 20 years ago." The participant explained that she was exasperated after hearing that comment. She confessed that she thought about leaving the school on many occasions. However, her friends on the volleyball team, which was racially diverse, provided support for her and kept her at the institution.

New Directions for Higher Education • DOI: 10.1002/he

Several participants, who could be classified as Afro-Latino/as, discussed that they were able to "pass as Black" because of their skin pigmentation. Racial passing is defined as identifying and presenting oneself as one race while denying ancestry of another (Khanna, 2010). It is important to point that the term *passing* was not something that we the researchers imposed on the participants. Rather, the participants used this term when they described their interactions with their Black peers on campus.

An example of a microinsult happened in the context of a student who "appeared" as one race but discussed "passing" for another. A Latino who identified as Puerto Rican but shared that he was able to pass as Black experienced a number of comments about his ethnicity. For example, this participant's friends often made negative comments about Puerto Ricans in his presence. When he later shared with them that he was Puerto Rican, they did not believe him. In fact, they asked him to say phrases in Spanish to "prove" his Puerto Rican authenticity. While on the surface this act can be viewed as a microassault because of the negative comments about other racial and ethnic groups, this can also be seen as a microinsult because the participant was asked to speak Spanish to validate his claim of being Latino. In a sense, this experience not only was rude, but also placed a psychological burden on the participant by forcing him to verify the legitimacy of being Latino.

Though much of the higher education literature on Latino/a students does not address the array of diversity that exists among this student demographic, Latino/as are very diverse in terms of ethnicities, skin tone, and geographic locations (Nuñez, Hoover, Pickett, Stuart-Carruthers, & Vázquez, 2013). While Afro-Latino/as are not mutually exclusive from Blacks (Seekle, 2008), once these participants' peers found out about their Latino heritage, they treated them differently. For example, a Latina participant indicated that because she was able to pass as Black, her peers on campus, with whom she was not extremely close, often forgot she was Latina and held conversations in front of her that ridiculed students of other races for wanting to join Black organizations or engage in interracial relationships. Despite these experiences, this participant explained that while she knew her peers did not mean any harm by their comments, she felt that the comments were negative.

A Latino participant, who also discussed the ability to pass as Black, had a different perspective. He stated that some of his peers on campus were ignorant about other cultures and that some of them held stereotypical views of Latino/as. Interestingly, this participant indicated that he came to this historically Black university to avoid being harassed because of his ethnicity. He assumed that since he looked Black and identified with Black people, he would be embraced by the Black community at this university. However, to some extent, his actual experience did not match his preconception.

NEW DIRECTIONS FOR HIGHER EDUCATION • DOI: 10.1002/he

It is interesting to note that the experiences of the Latino/a participants differed from the way that much of the literature has characterized the experiences of White students at HBCUs. For example, studies from Strayhorn (2010) and Hall and Closson (2005) have indicated that White students on the campuses of HBCUs have supportive relationships with members of the campus community in general and faculty in particular (Strayhorn, 2010). Although research has shown that White students at HBCUs experience no overt acts of racism (Nixon & Henry, 1991), some research has shown that White students at HBCUs have been called names, such as "Tom Cruise" or "White girl," which these students found to be racially offensive (Closson & Henry, 2008). Despite these experiences, researchers assert that these incidents are isolated and do not happen to all or a majority of White students at HBCUs. Moreover, similar to the views of Latino/a participants in the study, White students at HBCUs have also explained that faculty needed to be more inclusive and knowledgeable about other cultures in their teaching. Research has also suggested that White students as well as Latino/a students are expected to serve as spokespersons for their race when they are in classrooms at HBCUs (Peterson & Hamrick, 2009).

Although HBCUs have always been welcoming of racially diverse groups, the findings from the study of Latino/a students at this historically Black university suggest that all HBCUs could be more intentional in helping to facilitate a sense of belonging for this student demographic. The next section of this chapter delineates actions that leaders at HBCUs could take to achieve this goal.

Increasing the Sense of Belonging Among Latino/a Students at HBCUs

Based on the findings of this study, there are a number of relevant ways in which those in positions of leadership can improve facilitation of the sense of belonging for Latino/a students at HBCUs. The participants in the current study have provided insights that point to particular individuals or units within the university that can assist in creating a more welcoming environment. More specifically, these would involve the efforts of administrators, staff, and faculty in the following areas: (1) financial incentives (administrators), (2) activities and programs outside of the classroom (staff), and (3) discussions as facilitated in the classroom (faculty).

Sense of Belonging Through Financial Incentives.   Financial incentives to attend the historically Black university that was the site of the study were naturally a draw for the study participants. Given this finding, a sense of belonging can be facilitated by providing financial aid in the form of diversity scholarships for Latino/a students. Perhaps these diversity scholarships could also be provided throughout their college careers at the institution. The existence of these scholarships sends an encouraging message to the students that they are welcomed and recognized. Moreover, a strong

NEW DIRECTIONS FOR HIGHER EDUCATION • DOI: 10.1002/he

financial aid package with multiyear scholarship incentives not only lessens students' financial burdens but also increases their chances of persistence and eventual completion of their degrees.

Sense of Belonging Outside of the Classroom.   On another level, the activities and programs that take place outside of the classroom play an important role in facilitating a sense of belonging for Latino/a students at an HBCU. One of the prominent responses from participants involved their interactions with peers of different ethnicities on campus. Although participants did not consider these interactions a grave concern, conversations and statements about race still appeared to make them feel uneasy at times.

Student affairs professionals have the opportunity to address some of the racial microaggressions, more specifically microassaults and microinsults, through intentional programming and activities that affirm the culture and experiences of Latino/a students. For example, student affairs professionals involved in orientation can bring up these topics because they will interact with many of the new incoming populations of students. Orientation activities that are specific to recognizing and welcoming both students and parents from all races and ethnicities (e.g., Asian-American, Black, Latino/a, and White) to the college or university may help with setting a good foundation for the new students.

Student organizations have a vital role in facilitating a sense of belonging as well. Continuing to have specific student clubs for Latino/as will help them feel welcomed on campus. Additionally, these ethnic-specific clubs can encourage and facilitate interactions with other special-interest groups so they can establish better understandings of each other. One suggestion is that student affairs professionals who are in charge of student activities continue to encourage joint programs with various groups to help students interact and get to know each other on an informal and social basis.

Student affairs professionals who are involved with student support services, psychological services, and counseling services can encourage students to utilize their offices as well. Reaching out specifically to Latino/a students can help students adjust better to the HBCU campus environment. Also having a diverse staff in these offices may help students feel comfortable in approaching staff members with their academic and social concerns.

Residential life staff members at HBCUs have a tremendous opportunity to help by having programs that facilitate interactions with students because of the residential environments in which they live, eat, and interact with one another. These interactions do not necessarily have to be formal programs, but can be informal social settings that will make Latino/a students feel more comfortable in meeting and socializing with other students.

Most importantly, within these activities and programs, student affairs professionals play a vital role in facilitating these discussions, especially about racial microaggressions (Sue et al., 2007). How these discussions take place requires student affairs professionals to improve their knowledge and facilitation skills about racial dynamics and multicultural competence.

Sharpening these skills will in turn help all students, including Latino/a students, learn to improve their communication and understanding about racial microaggressions.

Sense of Belonging in the Classroom.   Just as it is important for programs to take place outside of the classroom, the discussions and activities within the classroom are vital. Faculty have a great opportunity to facilitate a sense of belonging for Latino/a students at HBCUs. Many of the participants mentioned that that they were left out of discussions because faculty seemed to exclude talking about other cultures in their classroom. Like student affairs professionals, faculty can also have an improved understanding of how they can facilitate a better sense of belonging for Latino/a students. One suggestion is to encourage more class discussion devoted to dialogue about other races, ethnicities, and cultures within the curriculum. These conversations can take the form of activities that allow students to share more about themselves with other students in their class, thus potentially helping students feel more comfortable speaking up in class. Creating a classroom environment that includes acknowledging differences and similarities may foster stronger feelings that students belong, which in return may allow students to be more willing to engage in dialogue about difficult topics with each other.

Because HBCUs have diverse environments, they are in a strong position to continue to find ways to facilitate a sense of belonging for Latino/a students and to encourage acknowledgment and recognition of Latino/a student populations at all levels of the college or university. Therefore, addressing the ways that a sense of belonging can be facilitated at various levels at the university will benefit not only the campus as a whole but also and most importantly the diverse student populations that attend.

Implications for Future Research

The current study revealed several implications for future research exploring the college-choice and on-campus experiences of Latino/a college students enrolled in an HBCU. First, this study found Latino/a students' college-choice processes were influenced by the opportunity to participate in collegiate athletics. Additional scholarly work should examine the unique lived experiences of Latino/a student athletes and investigate how these students interact with the larger HBCU campus community, both inside and outside of the classroom. Forthcoming studies may also consider the students' relationships with teammates to understand teammates' influence on campus engagement, involvement, and persistence. Moreover, future research could disaggregate participants by sports teams to gain an in-depth understanding of the similarities and differences of experiences between various athletic programs.

Academic programs and personal relationships with current HBCU students also played a large role in the college-choice process of Latino/a college students. Students were drawn to academic majors because of their reputations and their ability to teach profession-specific skills and competencies. To support college and departmental recruitment efforts, additional research should ask Latino/a students about their information-seeking behaviors and the opportunities or obstacles they encountered in gathering school or program information. Understanding the pipeline to particular programs can help academic units develop best practices in their recruitment and marketing strategies.

Financial support through diversity scholarships and proximity to home also facilitated Latino/a student enrollment in this historically Black university. In the future, researchers should consider the long-term implications of diversity scholarships and their long-term benefits. Additional work can examine the role these scholarships play in degree completion and graduate school enrollment.

This study also highlighted the need for further research on intergroup cultural differences within the Latino/a community. Afro-Latino participants in this study discussed their ability to pass as Black, which subsequently influenced their relationships with peers. Future research should investigate the nuanced experiences and perceptions of Latino/a subgroups (e.g., Mexican-American, Puerto Rican, Dominican, or Cuban) to reveal how different subpopulations interact with students, faculty, and peers at HBCUs. Further investigations should also consider the experiences of Latino/a students as they negotiate and navigate the intersectionality of their social identities (e.g., gender, sexual orientation, disability, etc.). Furthermore, increased Latino/a student enrollment warrants additional research on the perspectives and feelings of Black peers and HBCU alumni to uncover their perceptions on campus diversification. Their insight can provide clarification of how HBCU administrators and leaders can respond to concerns, if any, when enrolling more non-Black students.

Race relations, both inside and outside the classroom, emerged as a key finding for this study. Latino/a students described the microaggressions and microinsults they encountered from faculty members and Black peers. Future research should investigate the perceptions of HBCU faculty as they instruct more and more Latino/a students. Additional research should explore professors' responses to the increased diversity (e.g., course materials, discussion topics, and pedagogy), as well as any reservations or concerns they have about Latino/as enrolling in HBCUs. Scholars could also examine the experiences of HBCU student affairs administrators and how they perceive their role in promoting an inclusive learning environment and facilitating student development.

Given the emergence of microaggressions and microinsults, HBCUs could also consider administering campus climate surveys to gauge multiple stakeholders' points of view. Researchers should consider undertaking larger qualitative studies to examine the campus climate at multiple HBCU campuses. The cross-racial experiences of Latino/a students may differ depending upon the HBCU's governance, students, or academic programs (e.g., public, private, single-sex, faith-based, liberal arts), and the findings from these future studies can help guide the training and development of HBCU faculty and staff members as well as campus practices and policies.

Finally, this study was qualitative and the researchers did not employ a specific theoretical framework; they allowed the themes and subthemes to emerge from the data. A quantitative analysis of Latino/a college choice and on-campus experiences can provide patterns and potential explanations for student outcomes (e.g., sense of belonging). Further research may consider applying different theoretical lenses to study Latino/a college students enrolled in HBCUs. For example, critical race theories or college-choice theories can offer unique insight into these students' experiences. Adopting a purely grounded theory approach to develop a college-choice model for Latino/as in HBCUs can also benefit our understanding of this process.

References

Adams v. Richardson, 351 f.2d 636 (D.C. Cir. 1972).

Closson, R. B., & Henry, W. J. (2008). The social adjustment of undergraduate White students in the minority on an historically Black college campus. *Journal of College Student Development, 49*, 517–534.

Conrad, C. F., Brier, E. M., & Braxton, J. M. (1997). Factors contributing to the matriculation of White students in public HBCUs. *Journal for a Just and Caring Education, 3*(1), 37–62.

Gasman, M. (2009). *Diversity at historically Black colleges and universities.* Retrieved from http://diverseeducation.wordpress.com/2009/06/05/diversity-at-historically-black-colleges-and-universities/

Gasman, M. (2013). *The changing face of historically Black colleges and universities.* Philadelphia, PA: Center for Minority Serving Institutions, University of Pennsylvania.

Gasman, M., Lundy-Wagner, V., Ransom, T., & Bowman, N., III. (2010). *Unearthing promise and potential: Our nation's historically Black colleges and universities.* San Francisco, CA: Jossey-Bass.

Hall, B., & Closson, R. B. (2005). When the majority is the minority: White graduate students' social adjustment at a historically Black university. *Journal of College Student Development, 46*(1), 28–42.

Khanna, N. (2010). Passing as Black: Racial identity work among biracial Americans. *Journal of Black Studies, 73*(4), 380–397.

Lee, J. M., Jr. (2012). An examination of the participation of African American students in graduate education without public HBCUs. In R. T. Palmer, A. A. Hilton, & T. P. Fountaine (Eds.), *Black graduate education at historically Black colleges and universities: Trends, experiences, and outcomes* (pp. 61–82). Charlotte, NC: Information Age Publishing.

Lee, R. C. (2013, October 25). State college enrollment up overall, down among Latinos. *Houston Chronicle.* Retrieved from http://www.houstonchronicle.com/news/education/article/State-college-enrollment-up-overall-down-among-4927619.php

Nixon, H. L., & Henry, W. J. (1991). White students at the Black university: Their experiences regarding acts of racial intolerance. *Equity & Excellence in Education, 25*(2–4), 121–123.

NEW DIRECTIONS FOR HIGHER EDUCATION • DOI: 10.1002/he

Nuñez, A. M., Hoover, R. E., Pickett, K., Stuart-Carruthers, C., & Vázquez, M. (2013). *Latinos in higher education and Hispanic-serving institutions* [ASHE Higher Education Report, 39(1)]. San Francisco, CA: Jossey-Bass.

Paddock, A. (2013, May 17). Historically Black colleges are seeing an increase in White students. *The Washington Post*. Retrieved from http://www.washingtonpost.com/blog s/therootdc/post/historically-black-colleges-are-seeing-an-increase-of-white-students /2013/05/17/5a642f5e-bd80-11e2-89c9-3be8095fe767_blog.html

Palmer, R. T., Davis, R. J., & Maramba, D. C. (2011). The impact of family support on the success of Black men at an historically Black university: Affirming the revision of Tinto's theory. *Journal of College Student Development, 52*(5), 577–593.

Palmer, R. T., & Maramba, D. C. (in press-a). A delineation of Asian American and Latino/a students' experiences with faculty at an historically Black college and university. *Journal of College Student Development*.

Palmer, R. T., & Maramba, D. C. (in press-b). Racial microaggressions among Asian American and Latino/a students at an HBCU. *Journal of College Student Development*.

Palmer, R. T., & Wood, J. L. (Eds.). (2012). *Black men in college: Implications for HBCUs and beyond*. New York, NY: Routledge.

Patton, S. (2012, October 29). From cellblock to campus, one Black man defies the data. *The Chronicle of Higher Education*. Retrieved from http://chronicle.com/article /In-Terms-of-Gender/135294/

Peterson, R. D., & Hamrick, F. A. (2009). White, male, and "minority": Racial consciousness among White male undergraduates attending a historically Black university. *Journal of Higher Education, 80*(1), 34–58.

Seekle, C. R. (2008). *CRS report for Congress: Afro-Latinos in Latin America and considerations for U.S. policy*. Retrieved from http://www.fas.org/sgp/crs/row/RL32713.pdf

St. Philip's College. (2014). *2012–2013 annual fact book*. Retrieved from http://www .alamo.edu/uploadedFiles/SPC/Faculty_and_Staff/Departments_Non-Academic/Plan ning_and_Research/Files/SPC%20Fact%20Book%2012-13%20V4.pdf

Strayhorn, T. L. (2010). Majority as temporary minority: Examining the influence of faculty-student relationships on satisfaction among White undergraduates at historically Black colleges and universities. *Journal of College Student Development, 51*(5), 509–524.

Sue, D. W., Capodilupo, C. M., Torino, G. C., Bucceri, J. M., Holder, A. M. B., Nadal, K. L., & Esquilin, M. (2007). Racial microaggressions in everyday life: Implications for clinical practice. *American Psychologist, 62*(4), 271–286.

United States v. Fordice, 112 S. Ct. 2727 (1992).

ROBERT T. PALMER *is an associate professor of student affairs in the College of Community and Public Affairs at the State University of New York, Binghamton.*

DINA C. MARAMBA *is an associate professor of student affairs in the College of Community and Public Affairs at the State University of New York, Binghamton.*

TARYN OZUNA ALLEN *is an assistant professor of educational leadership and policy studies at the University of Texas at Arlington.*

RAMON B. GOINGS *is a doctoral candidate in urban educational leadership at Morgan State University, Baltimore, Maryland.*

This chapter highlights some of the extant literature on LGBT students at HBCUs and discusses some of the challenges they encounter at these institutions. Furthermore, it offers recommendations to help HBCUs be more intentional about creating a more affirming and inclusive campus environment for LGBT students.

The Role of HBCUs in Addressing the Unique Needs of LGBT Students

Steve D. Mobley Jr., Jennifer M. Johnson

Historically Black colleges and universities (HBCUs) have a rich history of being at the forefront and prominently championing controversial issues within American society, internationally, and in numerous Black communities. During the 1950s and 1960s, HBCUs and their students had a large presence in the Civil Rights movement. HBCU students also played a significant role in the Black Power movement in the 1970s. Also, in the 1980s and early 1990s, HBCU students were part of the fight against apartheid in South Africa. Overall, these institutions have played a critical role in creating spaces for civil rights and providing voice to those who encounter systematic oppression. Interestingly, HBCU communities and their students participated in these movements while often operating in very culturally conservative environments (Harper & Gasman, 2008). Consequently, a palpable tension persists within HBCUs as they continue to negotiate their commitment to the mission of racial uplift and their historically conservative campus environments.

Today, HBCUs find themselves grappling with a new civil rights issue when it comes to working with gay and lesbian students. Recent media reports portray HBCUs as actively suppressing the expression of gay and lesbian students—for example, limiting opportunities for these students to form student organizations or forcing them to conform to traditional forms of dress. Rather than encouraging students to walk in their own truth and embrace their authentic selves, many HBCUs compel students who identify as gay or lesbian to suppress these identities while on campus. The few campus interventions that seek to retain and engage gay and lesbian students are oftentimes limited in either scope or visibility.

New Directions for Higher Education, no. 170, Summer 2015 © 2015 Wiley Periodicals, Inc.
Published online in Wiley Online Library (wileyonlinelibrary.com) • DOI: 10.1002/he.20133

HBCUs and their students exist at a crossroads, an intersection of border spaces constituted by race, gender, and sexuality. We believe that HBCUs can no longer disregard the presence of lesbian, gay, bisexual, and transgender (LGBT) students on their campuses, nor can they continue to disregard the connections that exist between student identity, student sense of belonging, and college persistence. Now is the time for faculty and administrators at HBCUs to begin transformative dialogues that confront stereotypes and to challenge HBCU students, faculty, and administrators to extend conversations surrounding LGBT issues across their campuses and into the larger community. The ways that HBCUs provide support for their LGBT populations will undoubtedly impact higher education, Black communities, and society at large. We hope that this chapter will call HBCU communities, higher education scholars, and scholar-practitioners to action so that HBCUs may begin the necessary work to become inclusive campus communities for all of their students.

Looking Back

HBCUs have been recognized within higher education for their remarkable ability to provide their students with engaging academic and social environments (see, e.g., Fleming, 1984; Outcalt & Skewes-Cox, 2002). The existing HBCU research includes an array of topics. There is a substantial body of literature that focuses on the history, missions, and challenges of these institutions (see, e.g., Anderson, 1988; Brown & Davis, 2001). Other studies have compared the experiences of African-American students who attend HBCUs with those who attend predominantly White institutions (PWIs) (see, e.g., Fries-Britt & Turner, 2002). Previous scholarship has also examined the social adjustment, ethnic identity development, and academic success of HBCU students (see, e.g., Drezner, Villarreal, & Mobley, in press; Palmer & Davis, 2012). Taken together, HBCU research largely asserts that HBCU communities foster environments that allow their students to successfully integrate into the academic and social contexts of undergraduate student life through significant faculty contact, opportunities for campus leadership, and collegial peer interactions. While this assertion may be true, today HBCUs are grappling with their reputations of oftentimes being unreceptive and hostile to their students who identify with lesbian, gay, bisexual, or transgender (LGBT) communities (Gasman, Nguyen, & Kalam, 2013; Squire & Mobley, 2015; Strayhorn & Scott, 2012).

Challenges often manifest due to the conservative religious affiliations of both the students and these institutions. Many HBCUs were founded by religious organizations, including the Baptist, African Methodist Episcopal (AME), Catholic, and Presbyterian churches. Black church leaders are often cited for condemning LGBT populations within the Black community (Valera & Taylor, 2011). The conservative attitudes present within Black communities, including HBCU environments, have made it challenging for students who identify with LGBT communities to reconcile their sexual identities while in college (Kirby, 2011). The historical and contemporary religious affiliations that are inherent within HBCU communities present a tension of how and whether these institutions can and will take a reaffirming and nonjudgmental stance regarding the presence of Black LGBT communities on these campuses.

Research inquiry that explicitly seeks to examine the experiences of LGBT students who attend HBCUs is limited. There are a few existing studies that underscore the experiences of gay or bisexual males (see, e.g., Carter, 2013; Means & Jaeger, 2013; Patton, 2011; Strayhorn & Scott, 2012) and lesbian students (see, e.g., Patton & Simmons, 2008) who attend HBCUs and the challenges that they face during their undergraduate years. Overall, this scholarship paints a dichotomous picture of the experience of gay and lesbian students on these campuses. At one extreme, LGBT student experiences mirror previous research findings that students are able to develop positive peer relationships and engage in the academic and social communities on campus. On the other hand, this scholarship also emphasizes the conservative nature of HBCU environments and how many members of gay and lesbian communities often feel ignored and misrepresented. The strong religious and cultural pressure on HBCU campuses at times forces gay and lesbian students to feel as if they are silenced and invisible. These studies also reveal that gay and lesbian students on HBCU campuses may experience a sense of otherness both explicitly and implicitly during their interactions with their peers, administrators, and faculty. Within educational spaces individuals are often "othered" due to their race, ethnicity, gender, religion, sexual orientation, or socioeconomic status. This process involves a majority exercising their societal power dynamics to create distance and advantage (Lorde, 1996; Mojto, 2009; Tatum, 2000).

While this scholarship does highlight concerns relating to LGBT students who identify as gay and lesbian within the HBCU context, there is a dire need for additional critical inquiry in order for this discourse to progress. Even though HBCUs may be welcoming environments for many of their students who choose to attend, for those populations who openly identify as gay or lesbian, these environments may present struggles that mirror those that have challenged the African-American race in its fight for racial equality in White America. President Barack Obama declared during his 2013 inaugural address, "Our journey is not complete until our gay brothers and sisters are treated like anyone else under the law ... for if we are truly created equal, then surely the love we commit to one another must be equal as well" (Obama, 2013). In order to aptly begin this journey and answer this call for acceptance and equal rights, there must be more research and campus interventions that recognize the complexity and multiplicity of identity.

NEW DIRECTIONS FOR HIGHER EDUCATION • DOI: 10.1002/he

Responding Now to Impact the Future

Based on the extant literature and current policies and practices enacted by institutions of higher education, we offer recommendations on how HBCUs can holistically respond to and make sense of the needs of their students who are members of LGBT communities. HBCUs must work toward creating more inclusive and supportive campus environments for their diverse study bodies. In order to have substantial change with regard to transforming any particular HBCU into a more inclusive campus environment not only for LGBT students, but for students and staff seeking to express themselves on campus without fear of retribution, HBCU campus administrations must examine the roles they play in reinforcing and perpetuating heteronormative practices that privilege some while marginalizing others. These institutions must begin to reexamine their traditions and policies that impose strict rules that often inhibit individual student expression. HBCU communities must also begin to recognize how institutional practices that include dress codes, a lack of student health services geared toward gay and lesbian students, and same-sex housing policies often silence and "other" members of LGBT communities.

To begin this work, educators and administrators at HBCUs must intentionally structure conversations and provide forums where individuals from diverse communities can learn from their differences to build mutually respectful interactions. This can be achieved through: (1) developing campus resources for members of the LGBT community, (2) providing opportunities for students to engage in intergroup dialogue, and (3) encouraging the expansion of course offerings to include the voices and experiences of LGBT scholars and individuals. Our recommendations are not exhaustive but do provide a meaningful starting point for HBCU leaders to consider.

Developing Campus Resources for Members of the LGBT Community

The transition from high school to college can be particularly challenging for gay and lesbian students. While all students must learn to adjust to the academic responsibilities of college life, LGBT students are also often wrestling with the development of their sexual identities (Patton & Simmons, 2008). Support services for LGBT students are crucial during their time in college, as it is during this period that many individuals decide to come out and disclose their sexual identity to others. While HBCUs may provide an accepting environment for African Americans who choose to attend, those students who are openly gay or lesbian may be met with fear, suspicion, and distrust (Carter, 2013).

Within HBCU environments, gay and lesbian students oftentimes choose either to selectively disclose this aspect of their identity to supportive family members and friends or not to disclose at all. Black students who identify as gay or lesbian negotiate several oppressed identities at all times: the gay or lesbian persons they are internally and the heterosexual persons they present to the world on a daily basis (Cole & Guy-Sheftall, 2003; Patton & Simmons, 2008). Being able to find supportive services on campus would potentially help alleviate these concerns. This can be accomplished in several ways—by initiating "safe zones" on campus, promoting student-run LGBT organizations, and creating campus-based LGBT resource and research centers.

Safe Zones.   As a first step, if HBCU communities were to spearhead safe zone initiatives, these student-centered forums could be a valuable means of providing critical support for LGBT students throughout their college years. A safe zone (or safe space) refers to an on-campus space where LGBT students are able to seek support and affirmation and express their feelings and concerns without fear of harassment or violence. In order for this initiative to be enacted on HBCU campuses, administrators and faculty would need to receive safe zone training so that they could work with LGBT students through issues that are salient to them. Safe zone initiatives provide higher education communities with forums to educate students, faculty, and administrators on issues that are pertinent to LGBT students. Safe zones would undoubtedly assist HBCU campuses with issues surrounding the transition process into college that are unique to members of LGBT communities, and foster further immersion into the larger campus environment.

Fayetteville State University (FSU), an HBCU in North Carolina, is currently instituting safe zone programming. The purpose of the safe zone program at FSU is to "create an affirming and supportive campus climate through identifying and educating members of [the] campus community who are opened to and supportive of all individuals regardless of sexual orientation, gender identity, or gender expression" (Fayetteville State University, 2013). In other words, the program attempts to provide structured support to students and to refer students to appropriate resources for issues and concerns. This programming is a part of the university's efforts to raise awareness and education for LGBT students and their allies. It can serve as a model for other HBCUs that choose to initiate these programs. Safe zones have the unique opportunity to provide their LGBT populations with positive mentors/allies and cutting-edge programming that could inform the greater campus community about the lived experiences of its students who identify with LGBT communities.

Establishing Student-Run LGBT/Ally Organizations.   According to Astin (1993), peer groups significantly influence students' growth and development during their undergraduate years. These peer relationships are oftentimes forged through membership in student organizations. Currently, there are 21 HBCUs that have recognized LGBT/ally organizations on their campuses (Kirby, 2011). For example, Morehouse College has an organization (Safe Space) that has offered several campus forums and programs to discuss issues that are facing the Black gay community, including a weeklong series of events entitled "I Am a Man: Black Masculinity in America." The Human Rights Campaign (HRC), an LGBT advocacy group, has a key relationship with a number of HBCUs. Through its HBCU Initiative, the HRC trains students to build viable student-led LGBT-friendly organizations on campus, and works to mobilize students to engage discourse on LGBT issues on their respective campuses. Community partnerships and campus-wide stakeholders are critical to not only establishing these organizations but also ensuring their viability, perpetuity, and survival. These student-run organizations provide LGBT communities on HBCU campuses the opportunity to find comfort and the sense of belonging that fosters student retention and success (McMurtie, 2013).

LGBT Resource and Research Centers. The newly established LGBT resource and research centers on HBCU campuses have marked a pivotal step in creating campus cultures of acceptance and inclusion for LGBT students at HBCUs. These centers offer many benefits that include providing the necessary tools to educate an entire college or university community on critical LGBT issues, advocating for LGBT-inclusive institutional policies, and fostering positive campus atmospheres for LGBT students to feel safe and welcomed on campus. Bowie State University opened its Gender and Sexual Diversities Resource Center in 2012, making it the first HBCU to have a dedicated LGBT center. The center is intended to provide information, resources, and counseling to lesbian, gay, bisexual, transgender, questioning, intersex, and ally (LGBTQIA) students, and "increase awareness and affirmation of LGBTQIA individuals to reduce discrimination based on sexual orientation and gender identity" (Bowie State University, 2013). North Carolina Central University (NCCU) soon followed with the opening of its center. The goal of the North Carolina Central LGBTA center is "to create a place where everyone feels welcome" (North Carolina Central University, 2014), and it is part of a university effort to transform NCCU into a more inclusive campus environment. Located within the student union building, the center serves as a clearinghouse of information and resources and often cosponsors events and activities with student-run LGBT campus organizations to educate the wider campus community about LGBT-related issues.

LGBT resource and research centers have the capacity to substantially enrich campus communities. Kirby (2011) contends:

> The creation of LGBT resource and research centers at HBCUs is not simply about following the newest trend in higher education; it is about protecting the students who have chosen to attend those schools. ... HBCUs must decide to stop playing politics with religious denominations and alumni and do what is in the best interest of their students.

While the establishment of LGBT resource centers has marked a significant shift among HBCU communities, Kirby reports that there are only three HBCUs with active centers. If more HBCUs were to establish LGBT resource and research centers on their campuses, a strong message would be sent to broader HBCU and Black communities that now is the time to build bridges of acceptance and inclusion.

Facilitating Intergroup Dialogue

Due to the conservative campus cultures that characterize many HBCU communities, meaningful interactions between gay and heterosexual students have been routinely avoided. To remedy this, HBCUs could substantially benefit from the opportunity to introduce focused intergroup dialogues to their campuses. Zúñiga (2003) defines intergroup dialogue as a "face-to-face facilitated conversation between members of two or more social identity groups that strives to create new levels of understanding, relating, and action" (p. 9). These conversations would provide a forum for LGBT and heterosexual students to talk with one another across boundaries, dispel stereotypes, and move the campus toward an environment where all students could become positively engaged in the HBCU context. Bringing college students together to confront controversial subject matters is a complex and challenging endeavor. Effective dialogues will require considerable work by both facilitators and participants. Moreover, there will presumably be resistance to discussing controversial and sensitive topics such as sexual orientation or gender expression within an African-American context; therefore, facilitators must be aware of this resistance and actively challenge students to engage in these difficult conversations.

In 2011, Spelman College held the Audre Lorde Historically Black College and University Summit, which focused on LGBT issues within African-American and HBCU communities. This action-oriented conference created the opportunity for HBCU administrators, faculty, students, and alumni from 10 HBCUs to engage in dialogue about LGBT issues and offer recommendations about how HBCUs can establish open and inclusive environments for LGBT students and employees. Efforts like this are a potential first step for establishing ongoing opportunities to conduct dialogue across differences and to promote policies and practices that lead to systemic support for members of LGBT communities.

Creating Inclusive Academic Spaces and Expanding Course Offerings

As members of the academic community, HBCU faculty members have the opportunity to create inclusive intellectual spaces and expand course curricula that engage issues that are pertinent to LGBT communities. Currently, there are no HBCUs that offer LGBT studies as an academic major, minor, or certificate program. This void has been attributed to the negative repercussions associated with institutional backlash, faculty fear of being seen as confrontational, faculty apprehension of being "outed" as gay or lesbian, and (for junior faculty) potential refusal of tenure (Spelman College Women's Research and Resource Center, 2011). As a result, there are limited academic opportunities for students to examine issues surrounding gender and sexuality. Scholars at the Spelman College Women's Research and Resource Center (2011) contend:

> In contexts where same-sex sexuality remains taboo, presumably supported by religious dictates that mark it as such, pervasive ideas about heterosexual morality or heteronormativity usurp the place of curricular engagement in ways that make it difficult for LGBT students to locate themselves within a robust intellectual legacy. (p. 19)

There have been a few instances where gay and lesbian authors are included in classroom discussions and course topics, but their identification with LGBT communities is seldom mentioned and often goes without interrogation (Spelman College Women's Research and Resource Center, 2011). Including the voices of acclaimed scholars such as Alice Walker, James Baldwin, Audre Lorde, and Langston Hughes in the classroom *and* recognizing the LGBT themes throughout their work would provide spaces that challenge and renegotiate the notions of what it means to be Black and gay or lesbian in the broader societal context.

While there is a lack of LGBT studies curricula within HBCU contexts, at some HBCUs the topics of gender and sexuality are being addressed in select course offerings. In 1981, Spelman College introduced the women's studies minor, and in 1996 it expanded the program into a major in comparative women's studies (Spelman College Women's Research and Resource Center, 2011). Spelman is the only HBCU with a women's studies major. This department currently offers courses that broach matters that are inclusive of key LGBT issues, including a course titled "Black Queer Studies." Morehouse College also recently offered a course titled "A Genealogy of Black LGBT Culture and Politics" that was taught remotely by a Yale University professor. The campus's gay/straight alliance organization partnered with Yale to make this course offering a reality. It is very encouraging to see HBCUs taking steps to develop courses and expand their curricula. Other HBCUs should use these examples to further develop their academic spaces and move forward so they can aptly address LGBT history, issues, and culture.

Moving Forward

Within the past decade, HBCUs have begun to recognize the unique needs of their LGBT communities. Although HBCUs have been slow to fully embrace the LGBT students who are present on their campuses, it is evident that there have been significant strides in examining campus climates so that

LGBT students may truly feel welcomed. For far too long, HBCUs have communicated to LGBT students that as long as they are not too "out" with expressing their sexual identities, then everything is okay. The new and emerging initiatives highlighted in this chapter convey great potential and demonstrate how HBCU communities are indeed beginning to recognize and address the challenges and potential barriers to college persistence that LGBT students encounter during their time in college. Still, there is work to be done.

Many HBCUs continue to prevent their students from establishing permanent student-run LGBT/ally organizations and have failed to facilitate campus-wide programs that highlight LGBT issues. Because most HBCUs lack an infrastructure of support for their LGBT students, progress at many institutions comes because of the work of a few activists. It is crucial that student-run organizations and student services expand to other HBCUs so that LGBT students can be embraced and aided during their time within HBCU contexts. Each year, students voluntarily withdraw from institutions of higher education, not due to poor academic performance but due to feelings of isolation or alienation within the academic or social spaces of campus. Moving forward, it will be imperative for HBCU communities to embrace the diverse students who are matriculating on their campuses, especially their students who also identify as gay, lesbian, bisexual, or transgender. Future initiatives and interventions must critically examine LGBT issues and propose effective solutions. Understanding the experiences of marginalized students and the meanings that these students attach to their experiences is paramount in aiding their growth, development, and success.

References

Anderson, J. D. (1988). *The education of Blacks in the South*. Chapel Hill, NC: University of North Carolina Press.

Astin, A. (1993). *What matters in college: Four critical years revisited*. San Francisco, CA: Jossey-Bass.

Bowie State University. (2013). *Gender and Sexual Diversities Resource Center*. Retrieved from http://www.bowiestate.edu/campus-life/division-of-student-affairs/gender-and-sexual-diversities-/

Brown, M. C., II, & Davis, E. J. (2001). The historically Black college as social contract, social capital, and social equalizer. *Peabody Journal of Education, 76*(1), 31–49.

Carter, B. A. (2013). Nothing better or worse than being Black, gay, and in the band: Qualitative examination of gay undergraduates participating in historically Black college or university marching bands. *Journal of Research in Music Education, 61*(1), 26–43.

Cole, J., & Guy-Sheftall, B. (2003). *Gender talk: The struggle for women's equality in African American communities*. New York, NY: Ballantine Books.

Drezner, N. D., Villarreal, R. C., & Mobley, S. D., Jr. (in press). Choosing not to sit together: Experiences of White honors students at a public HBCU. In T. L. Strayhorn, M. S. Williams, and D. Tillman-Kelly (Eds.), *Creating new possibilities for the future of HBCUs with research*. Charlotte, NC: Information Age Publishing.

NEW DIRECTIONS FOR HIGHER EDUCATION • DOI: 10.1002/he

Fayetteville State University. (2013). Safe Zone Office. Retrieved from http://www
.uncfsu.edu/studentaffairs/safe-zone

Fleming, J. (1984). *Blacks in college: A comparative study of students' success in Black and White institutions*. San Francisco, CA: Jossey-Bass.

Fries-Britt, S. V., & Turner, B. (2002). Uneven stories: Successful Black collegians at a Black and White campus. *Review of Higher Education, 25*(3), 313–339.

Gasman, M., Nguyen, T.-H., & Kalam, S. (2013). Black undergraduates at historically Black colleges and universities and multiple identities. In T. L. Strayhorn (Ed.), *Living at the intersections: Social identities and Black collegians* (pp. 221–236). Charlotte, NC: Information Age Publishing.

Harper, S. R., & Gasman, M. (2008). Consequences of conservatism: Black male students and the politics of historically Black colleges and universities. *The Journal of Negro Education, 77*(4), 336–351.

Kirby, V. D. (2011). The Black closet: The need for LGBT resource and research centers on historically Black campuses. *LGBTQ Policy Journal at the Harvard Kennedy School.* Retrieved from http://isites.harvard.edu/icb/icb.do?keyword=k78405&pageid=icb
.page414497

Lorde, A. (1996). There is no hierarchy of oppression. In J. Andrzejewski (Ed.), *Oppression and social justice: Critical frameworks* (p. 51). Boston, MA: Pearson Custom.

McMurtie, B. (2013, October 28). Spurred by activists, HBCUs expand their services for gay students. *The Chronicle of Higher Education.* Retrieved from https://chronicle.com/article/Spurred-by-Activists-HBCUs/142559/

Means, D. R., & Jaeger, A. J. (2013). Black in the rainbow: "Quaring" the Black gay male student experience at historically Black universities. *Journal of African American Males in Education, 4*(2), 124–141.

Mojto, A. L. M. (2009). *Breaking the cycle of hate: A phenomenological study of teachers' lived experiences as both other and otherer* (Unpublished doctoral dissertation). University of Maryland, College Park. Retrieved from ProQuest Digital Dissertations (304922487).

North Carolina Central University. (2014). *Lesbian, Gay, Bisexual, Transgender and Ally Resource Center.* Retrieved from www.nccu.edu/lgbta/index.cfm

Obama, B. H. (2013, January). *2013 Presidential Inauguration Address.* Washington, DC.

Outcalt, C. L., & Skewes-Cox, T. E. (2002). Involvement, interaction, and satisfaction: The human environment at HBCUs. *Review of Higher Education, 25*(3), 331–347.

Palmer, R. T., & Davis, R. J. (2012). Diamond in the rough: The impact of a remedial program on college access and opportunity for Black males at a historically Black institution. *Journal of College Student Retention, 13*(4), 407–430.

Patton, L. D. (2011). Perspectives on identity, disclosure, and the campus environment among African American gay and bisexual men at one historically Black college. *Journal of College Student Development, 52*(1), 77–100.

Patton, L. D., & Simmons, S. L. (2008). Exploring complexities of multiple identities in a Black college environment. *Negro Educational Review, 59*(3–4), 197–215.

Spelman College Women's Research and Resource Center. (2011). *Facilitating campus climates of pluralism, inclusivity, and progressive change at HBCUs.* Atlanta, GA: Spelman College.

Squire, D., & Mobley, S. D., Jr. (2015). Negotiating race and sexual orientation in the college choice process of Black gay males. *The Urban Review.* Advance online publication. doi:10.1007/s11256-014-0316-3

Strayhorn, T. L., & Scott, J. A. (2012). Coming out of the dark: Black gay men's experiences at historically Black colleges and universities. In R. T. Palmer & J. L. Wood (Eds.), *Black men in college: Implications for HBCUs and beyond* (pp. 26–40). New York, NY: Routledge.

Tatum, B. D. (2000). The complexity of identity: "Who am I?" In M. Adams, W. J. Blumenfeld, R. Castaneda, H. W. Hackman, M. L. Peters, & X. Zúñiga (Eds.), *Readings for diversity and social justice* (pp. 9–14). New York, NY: Routledge.

Valera, P., & Taylor, T. (2011). Hating the sin but not the sinner: A study about heterosexism and religious experiences among Black men. *Journal of Black Studies, 42*(1), 106–122.

Zúñiga, X. (2003). Bridging differences through dialogue. *About Campus, 7*(6), 8–16.

STEVE D. MOBLEY JR. is a PhD candidate within the higher education concentration in the College of Education at the University of Maryland, College Park.

JENNIFER M. JOHNSON, PhD, is an assistant professor in the Department of Teaching, Learning, and Professional Development at Bowie State University, Bowie, Maryland.

7

This chapter discusses how diversity has typically been presented in the HBCU scholarly work, and explores how HBCUs may connect more effectively with the American postsecondary policy agenda.

Coming Out of the Shadows: Rethinking the Education Policy Agenda for Diversity and HBCUs

Valerie C. Lundy-Wagner

Historically Black colleges and universities (HBCUs) have a unique place in American higher education and Black education in particular (Gasman, Lundy-Wagner, Ransom, & Bowman, 2010). In fact, HBCUs have contributed disproportionately to the diversification of Black professional, political, and economic opportunity, both in employing and in educating African-American men and women (Lundy-Wagner & Gasman, 2011; Perna, 2001). In addition, the HBCU postsecondary contributions have had numerous effects on ethnic/racial diversity in the military, government, business, and science (see, e.g., Gasman et al., 2010; Solórzano, 1995). These 19th- and 20th-century gains, however, have failed to contribute to or inform the larger American higher education agenda. In fact, some might suggest that HBCUs have been unable to leverage their relevance at the state level or in the higher education policy arena overall. Such exclusion has likely contributed to unresolved negative perceptions and general skepticism about the relevance of HBCUs.

A major goal of this chapter is to demonstrate the policy relevance of HBCUs within a discussion about diversity. First, the chapter describes traditional treatment of diversity within the HBCU scholarly work and why that work may be limited. Subsequent sections present alternate considerations of diversity at HBCUs, using the extant research to connect timely issues to this unique subset of institutions. The ultimate goal of this chapter is to shed light on issues and methodologies that may help HBCUs better articulate their contributions at local, state, and national levels through rigorous consideration of data. The chapter includes recommendations that should enable HBCUs to leverage their context-based assets to promote short- and longer-term viability, and therefore should be informative to education

NEW DIRECTIONS FOR HIGHER EDUCATION, no. 170, Summer 2015 © 2015 Wiley Periodicals, Inc.
Published online in Wiley Online Library (wileyonlinelibrary.com) • DOI: 10.1002/he.20134

policy researchers who have little understanding of where HBCUs might fit into their and their colleagues' work.

Charting the Landscape

Most of the research and rhetoric surrounding HBCUs, diversity, and education policy incorporate descriptive statistics to justify the post–civil rights relevance of HBCUs or engender support for them, a trend noted by Lundy-Wagner and Gasman (2011). For example, the early seminal work by Allen (1992) and Fleming (1984) compared Black students' academic and social experiences in HBCUs and predominantly White institutions (PWIs). Using different samples, both authors essentially concluded that African-American students in HBCU environments were more satisfied socially and performed better academically than their counterparts at PWIs. This and similar research provided HBCU proponents with evidence that, in general, HBCUs were a better choice for African-American students than PWIs. Ultimately, this type of work provided some justification for HBCUs within the American postsecondary arena but did not place HBCUs at the decision-making table.

The mostly descriptive work on HBCU contributions to Black postsecondary educational attainment is present in policy research about exemplars of success (Harmon, 2012). While some researchers have built upon the early scholarship (see, e.g., Conrad, Brier, & Braxton, 1997), most of this work has not matured in ways that are comparable to other education policy research (e.g., employing causal inference). Furthermore, the research on the economic benefits of attending an HBCU—a strand of research that might incorporate rigorous research methods—has revealed mixed results (see, e.g., Constantine, 1995; Erhrenberg & Rothstein, 1994). As a result, with only a few exceptions, HBCUs and other minority-serving institutions have remained largely invisible within the education policy arena because of both substantive and methodological limitations.

College Access and Diversity

Most research on HBCUs and diversity focuses on students. Prior to the 1960s, HBCUs educated virtually all African-Americans pursuing a postsecondary education (Anderson, 1988). As Black school choice increased, HBCUs have continued to be exemplars in diversifying the college-educated American population. Further, since HBCUs mainly comprise 4-year colleges and universities, they have played an important role in diversifying the bachelor's degree–holding population. As of 2013, although HBCUs represented 3% of all postsecondary institutions, they educated upward of 16% of all African-American undergraduates (National Center for Education Statistics, 2013). HBCUs also have an important role in African-American graduate and professional credential receipt. In fact, during 2007–2008 HBCUs awarded only 1.3% of all master's and 1.8% of all first professional degrees, yet they conferred 11% of Black master's and first professional degrees earned (Lundy-Wagner, 2013a).

While HBCUs have undoubtedly played a critical role in African-American postsecondary education, recent research indicates that they are important providers of education for other students as well. Whereas prior to the mid-1960s, HBCUs almost exclusively educated African-American students, recent ethnic and racial breakdowns of HBCU enrollment reveal a new average undergraduate composition: 76% Black, 13% White, 3% Latina/o, and 1% Asian-American students (Gasman, 2013). These institutions' graduate and professional degree programs are also diverse, often enrolling White and other non-Black students (Provasnik, Shafer, & Snyder, 2004).

Besides the contributions of HBCUs to diversity in terms of ethnicity and race, they also disproportionately educate a significant number of low-income students (as measured by number and/or proportion of federal Pell grant recipients). Gasman (2013) highlights the substantially higher percentage of Pell grant recipients at HBCUs compared to PWIs in Mississippi (59.7% versus 44.8%) and in North Carolina (69.8% versus 27.5%).

HBCUs are also well known for diversifying various professional fields; the contribution of HBCUs in preparing Black doctoral degree recipients and college and university faculty is well known (Lundy-Wagner, Vultaggio, & Gasman, 2013; Perna, 2001). The role of HBCUs in Black teacher preparation (Gasman et al., 2010) and in increasing the number of Blacks in the science, technology, engineering, and mathematics (STEM) pipeline is also notable (Lundy-Wagner, 2013b; Perna et al., 2009). In fact, Lundy-Wagner notes that if HBCUs doubled their production of African-American men in STEM fields annually, despite representing only 3% of postsecondary institutions, they would double the Black male STEM pipeline. Characterizations of HBCU students by ethnicity and race, low-income status, and academic field provide undisputable descriptive evidence for why HBCUs matter for diversity in American postsecondary education.

Faculty and Staff Diversity at HBCUs

HBCUs also employ ethnically/racially diverse faculty. In fact, research shows that for many years the faculties at HBCUs have included African Americans and foreign-born Africans as well as Asians, Latino/as, and Whites (National Center for Education Statistics, 2013). In the early days, HBCUs had White faculty and administrators out of necessity for social and economic reasons, but they and other non-Blacks have been employed on HBCU campuses in more recent years to meet instructional needs (Foster, 2001). Some estimate that by the early 2000s, 25% or more of the HBCU faculty was White (Foster, 2001).

NEW DIRECTIONS FOR HIGHER EDUCATION • DOI: 10.1002/he

In addition to having diverse faculties, HBCUs also contribute to the diversification of the academy beyond their own walls (Solórzano, 1995; Trower & Chait, 2002; Wolf-Wendel, 1998). In fact, each of these studies found that more Black individuals who earned doctorates and eventually entered academe had received their baccalaureate degrees from HBCUs than from PWIs. Also, Perna (2001) found that 9% of full-time African-American faculty earned their doctorates from HBCUs and that more than half of them returned to their degree-granting institution as teaching faculty. Taken together, the research shows that HBCUs play an important role in terms of the undergraduate origins of Black doctoral degree recipients, employment of Black doctoral degree holders, and representation of other ethnic/racial groups among their faculties.

A Contemporary Perspective

While the literature on student enrollments, completions, and faculty diversity at, or as a result of, HBCUs is important, there are a number of ways that the extant research can appropriate a more expansive notion of diversity to showcase their strengths, solicit support, and articulate their relevance within the education policy arena. This section presents additional information that may help shed light on how HBCUs are relevant to policy discussions related to diversity.

Desegregation and Diversity.   Despite the contributions HBCUs have made to college access and diversity, desegregation plans resulting from the civil rights era are rarely mentioned; however, they play an important role in public HBCUs' viability (Gasman et al., 2010). With the passage of the Civil Rights Act, *Brown v. Board of Education*, and other legal actions, African Americans were legally empowered with school choice at the primary, secondary, and postsecondary levels. Desegregation for PWIs meant enrolling African Americans (and other non-Whites); for HBCUs, desegregation meant increasing their number of White students, despite the fact that HBCUs never had discriminatory admissions policies. One of the consequences of state desegregation cases was the perceived need to improve the quality of public HBCU academic programs so that non-Blacks would indeed enroll (Gasman et al., 2010; Palmer, Davis, & Gasman, 2011). In many cases, this effort contributed to states revisiting the duplication of programs at public HBCUs and local PWIs, and ensuring that HBCUs had a foothold on a certain proportion of higher education programs that would be desirable to White and other non-Black students.

Therefore, most of the *legal* issues surrounding student diversity at HBCUs pertain to increasing White undergraduate enrollment in order to meet outdated and racist desegregation goals. Despite this conceptual blunder (i.e., ignoring the American citizenry not classified as White, non-Hispanic, or Black), HBCUs are poised to maintain and increase their contributions to diversifying the bachelor's degree–holding population.

Evidence shows that not only do HBCUs disproportionately educate African-American students, but increasingly they are educating significant numbers of Latina/o and Asian-American students as well (Gasman, 2013; Palmer & Maramba, in press-a, in press-b). Yet, it is unknown whether individual institutions or HBCUs as a group have committed to definitive recruitment strategies that attract a wide variety of ethnic/racial students to attend (Black Issues, 2000). Therefore, in order to better reflect their ongoing contributions to increasing diversity, HBCUs, and especially public HBCUs, should seriously consider legal or legislative efforts toward removing or modifying state mandates that desegregation efforts focus primarily or only on White students as a representative measure of desegregation. HBCUs are also poised to clarify the concepts of desegregation and educational equity that appear to have been convoluted over time.

Resegregation and HBCUs.   On the one hand, HBCUs have been forced to address the aforementioned issues of desegregation. Yet, on the other hand, they exist within an American postsecondary landscape that Carnevale and Strohl (2013) soberly describe as becoming more segregated for ethnic/racial and low-income students. While that report does not discuss HBCUs specifically, the issues Carnevale and Strohl highlight provide some justification for a more substantive HBCU contribution to accountability efforts within the college completion agenda.

For example, President Obama's Postsecondary Institution Ratings System (PIRS) aims to advance institutional accountability, enhance transparency, and improve student and family college-related decision making. While the PIRS was conceptualized to help students and families, it does not take account the ways that institutions like HBCUs provide value-added benefits to socioeconomically disadvantaged students *despite* being under-resourced (see, e.g., Carmichael, Labat, Hunter, Privett, & Sevenair, 1993). That is, if underresourced HBCUs that enroll students with a wide variety of academic preparation are compared to better-resourced institutions with more prepared undergraduates, then HBCUs may very well be disadvantaged. In effect, the PIRS may damage HBCUs as a viable postsecondary choice for Black and non-Black students by underreporting the gains they facilitate with students if the PIRS does not account for the historical and ongoing disparities in funding that many HBCUs experience (see, e.g., Brady, Eatman, & Parker, 2000) or how their undergraduate populations may be unique. Accountability policies must be thoroughly examined, ideally by HBCU and other postsecondary leaders, in order to appropriately contextualize how these policies may disproportionately affect HBCUs, and also to highlight potential needed policy or procedural modifications.

HBCUs and Predominantly Black Institutions.   HBCUs undoubtedly educate a disproportionate number of African-American students in 4-year colleges and universities. Yet, as of 2008/2010, the predominantly Black institution (PBI) minority-serving designation was established. Among other criteria, institutions eligible for the PBI designation must have Black undergraduate enrollments of 40% or more. In 2010 and 2011, amounts of approximately $10 million and $9 million were awarded to 23 and 35 PBIs, respectively, to better support African-American students' postsecondary success. The vast majority of the institutions eligible for PBI designation and receiving PBI funds were 2-year colleges. In fact, only 2 of 23 in 2010 and 6 of 35 in 2011 were 4-year institutions.

Although PBIs do not have the same historical mission and context of HBCUs, they are quite similar in their relatively large African-American enrollment. Given the rather flat postsecondary enrollment in recent years that is also anticipated for the near future, HBCUs may consider partnering with PBIs and perhaps other minority-serving institutions (MSIs) to develop enrollment pipelines. PBIs and other MSIs may represent an important pathway for African-American students unfamiliar with HBCUs or unable to consider enrolling in HBCUs due to lack of academic preparedness, costs, or other reasons. Given the challenges many community college students have in persisting long enough to receive a credential or to transfer (see, e.g., Jaggars & Xu, 2010), this may be an opportunity for HBCUs to connect themselves to community colleges that have similar demographic profiles and promote their own mission of educating African-Americans.

Dual Enrollment

Another way that HBCUs can secure a place in state education policy agendas is to offer dual enrollment programs. These programs provide high school students with the opportunity to learn firsthand about the social and academic expectations of college. Historically, dual enrollment programs have focused on the highest-achieving students, providing them with incentives to enroll in the postsecondary institution such as college credit, time away from high school, and an increased level of independence. Yet, in recent years, these programs have expanded to include students of lower and middle academic-achievement levels and have achieved positive outcomes (Wilson, 2009).

In general, dual enrollment programs are considered a benefit to students, institutions, and society. In one study, students in dual enrollment programs were more likely to graduate from high school, make a transition to a 4-year college, persist in postsecondary education, and accumulate more college credits; they were also less likely to need basic skills courses (Hughes, Rodriguez, Edwards, & Belfield, 2012). These programs may also be practical for enrollment management reasons. Many HBCUs are tuition-driven, and changes in enrollment can therefore significantly affect revenue. Dual enrollment can potentially open HBCUs up to receive supplemental tuition for participating high school students. Dual enrollment could also become a strong predictor of local student matriculation, as proximity matters (Turley, 2009). Despite the various potential benefits, successful implementation of dual enrollment is not an easy task and would require that

HBCUs cultivate and maintain relationships with high schools and state policy makers.

Underprepared Students' Postsecondary Access.   Given HBCUs' typically open-door admissions policies, more work is needed to contextualize how these institutions fit into remedial (or developmental) education policy. According to some researchers, upward of 60% of students entering community colleges begin as developmental students (Bailey, Jeong, & Cho, 2010). Although most HBCUs are not community colleges, those with open-door policies are attractive for students interested in college who do not meet the highest levels of college preparedness. In recent years, as part of the national movement toward institutional efficiency, developmental education has been moved out of public 4-year institutions and become largely assigned to public 2-year or community colleges. While this seemingly race-neutral policy is aimed at improving statewide postsecondary institutional accountability, it is possible that the policy change has diverted some underprepared students who would have applied to and enrolled at a four-year HBCU to community colleges—postsecondary institutions that are known to have poor persistence and graduation rates, especially for minority students (see, e.g., Bailey, Jenkins, & Leinbach, 2005). Policy research examining whether college application and college-going rates have changed among students who typically would have enrolled at HBCUs is necessary in states where such policy changes have been enacted (e.g., North Carolina and Florida). If HBCUs are doing a better job at preparing academically underprepared students than community colleges in terms of moving students through the undergraduate experience, then blanket policies removing remedial offerings from open-access 4-year institutions should be revisited with particular attention to HBCUs.

The Southern Education Foundation (Parker, 2012) also highlights the influence of state funding for developmental education programs. For example, the foundation notes that in one Arkansas HBCU, 93% of entering students are referred to developmental education. With reductions in state allocations for remedial curricula, it's clear that this particular institution will be significantly affected in its ability to serve students. Again, since many HBCUs are tuition-driven and rely heavily on state and federal funding, understanding the financial role developmental education policy plays in HBCU fiscal stability is also critical.

Financial Aid.   Another accountability issue that HBCUs are poised to inform is postsecondary financial aid. In fact, in 2011 in response to egregious levels of borrowing for college, the Obama administration changed the eligibility criteria for parent PLUS loans, particular federal loans that are a vehicle available to dependent students' parents. According to Doubleday (2013):

> Until 2011, applicants were approved for a PLUS loan as long as they were
> not more than 90 days delinquent on any debt, and did not have any

foreclosures, bankruptcies, tax liens, wage garnishments, or student-loan de-
faults in the past five years. Under the new standards, unpaid debts in collection and student loans written off as unpayable in the previous five years also
count against applicants. (para. 5)

Despite the seemingly equitable changes in PLUS loan eligibility for all
borrowers, HBCUs and African-American students were disproportionately
negatively affected. Of the 400,000 PLUS loan denials, 7% were for students
attending HBCUs, even though HBCUs represent only 3% of postsecondary
institutions. In addition, HBCUs, most of whom are tuition-driven, saw notable enrollment declines and concomitant decreases in revenue (Doubleday, 2013). This change resulted in many effects, at least one that is known
to hinder students' ability to earn credit and credentials: stopping out. As
some researchers have shown, significant changes in financial aid or enrollment status can have catastrophic effects on completion, even for students who are in good academic standing (see, e.g., DesJardins, Ahlburg, &
McCall, 2002). In this case, federal financial aid policies did not acknowl-
edge historical and ongoing racial discrimination in access to credit or
disparities in wealth by race (Elliott & Beverly, 2011) and the disproportionate role race plays in HBCUs providing access for their primarily
African-American student bodies.

Implications

Although HBCUs have been a primary gateway for African Americans to
earn 4-year degrees, there may be a number of threats to maintaining this
pattern. That is, various federal, state, institutional, and local policies may
be diverting students, including academically underprepared and socioeconomically disadvantaged students, away from HBCUs. By embracing an expansive definition of diversity that is attentive to ethnicity/race beyond the
Black-White paradigm and enrollment numbers, HBCUs are indeed poised
to become more involved with the postsecondary policy agenda. While increasing enrollment of White and other non-Black students is an important starting point, there are a variety of other ways for HBCUs to become
engaged:

- Develop explicit and coherent policies for student recruitment. This
  might include recruitment of non-Black students but also high school students via a dual enrollment program, students in nearby states, students
  in states with anti-affirmative-action sentiment, and non-Black American
  and international students from a variety of ethnic/racial and socioeconomic backgrounds.
- Conduct research on the role HBCUs play in low-income, first-
  generation, and minority postsecondary access. Due to the historical
  purpose of HBCUs, their focus on Black students should continue, but

understanding how other marginalized students fare by having HBCUs as a choice is also necessary.

- Conduct research on federal, state, and local policies. For example, exploring the role that developmental education plays at HBCUs in terms of student enrollment, curriculum, faculty expertise, state and federal funding, as well as outcomes may be an important way to actively engage in state policy making.

- Finally, there is a rather disjointed body of research and policy on the economic impact of HBCUs (see, e.g., Humphreys & Korb, 2005). More research on this issue should be conducted to further highlight the economic role HBCUs play in their local and regional areas.

Conclusion

HBCUs continue to play an important role in the American postsecondary landscape for both African-American and other socioeconomically disadvantaged students. While a dated Black-White social and legal paradigm of diversity has dominated, HBCUs should strive for a more expansive and inclusive perspective. HBCUs have myriad opportunities to play an important role in setting the education policy agenda via diversity. This chapter has discussed issues like college access, dual enrollment, remedial education, financial aid, and the lingering issues related to de jure and de facto segregation as topics into which HBCUs can insert themselves. Although the typical descriptive research on HBCU contributions to enrollment, completions, and faculty diversity is important, these other influential topics provide an opportunity for HBCUs to engage with the larger American agenda for educational equity. Diversity policy at HBCUs should not focus only on enrolling White students; rather it should focus on sustaining a legacy of equity that recognizes contemporary issues (e.g., ethnic/racial demographic shifts, variation in academic preparedness, and socioeconomic diversity) and highlights the relevance of HBCUs to American education and specifically to Black education.

References

Allen, W. R. (1992). The color of success: African-American college student outcomes at predominantly White and historically Black public colleges and universities. *Harvard Educational Review*, 62(1), 26–44.

Anderson, J. D. (1988). *The education of Blacks in the South, 1860–1935*. Chapel Hill, NC: University of North Carolina Press.

Bailey, T., Jenkins, D., & Leinbach, T. (2005). *Community college low-income and minority student completion study: Descriptive statistics from the 1992 high school cohort*. New York, NY: Community College Research Center.

Bailey, T., Jeong, D. W., & Cho, S. (2010). Referral, enrollment, and completion in developmental education sequences in community colleges. *Economics of Education Review*, 29, 255–270.

Black Issues. (2000, November 9). Georgia wants more White students to enroll at state's HBCUs. *Diverse: Issues in Higher Education*.

Brady, K., Eatman, T., & Parker, L. (2000). To have or not to have? A preliminary analysis of higher education funding disparities in the post-*Ayers v. Fordice* era: Evidence from critical race theory. *Journal of Education Finance, 25*(3), 297–322.

Carmichael, J. W., Labat, D. D., Hunter, J. T., Privett, J. A., & Sevenair, J. P. (1993). Minorities in the biological sciences: The Xavier success story and some implications. *BioScience, 43*(3), 564–569.

Carnevale, A. P., & Strohl, J. (2013). *Separate and unequal: How higher education reinforces the intergenerational reproduction of White racial privilege*. Retrieved from https://georgetown.app.box.com/s/zhi9ilgzba9ncmr16ral

Conrad, C. F., Brier, E. M., & Braxton, J. M. (1997). Factors contributing to the matriculation of White students in public HBCUs. *Journal for a Just and Caring Education, 3*(1), 37–62.

Constantine, J. M. (1995). The effects of attending historically Black colleges and universities on future wages of Black students. *Industrial and Labor Relations Review, 48*(3), 531–546.

DesJardins, S. L., Ahlburg, D. A., & McCall, B. P. (2002). Simulating the longitudinal effects of changes in financial aid on student departure from college. *Journal of Human Resources, 37*(3), 653–679.

Doubleday, J. (2013, October 7). With parents denied loans, students scramble at HBCUs. *The Chronicle of Higher Education*. Retrieved from http://chronicle.com /article/Without-Federal-PLUS-Loans/142147/

Ehrenberg, R. G., & Rothstein, D. S. (1994). Do historically Black institutions of higher education confer unique advantages on Black students? An initial analysis. In R. G. Ehrenberg (Ed.), *Choices and consequences: Contemporary policy issues in education* (pp. 89–137). Ithaca, NY: ILR Press.

Elliott, W., & Beverly, S. (2011). The role of savings and wealth in reducing "wilt" between expectations and college attendance. *Journal of Children and Poverty, 17*(2), 165–185.

Fleming, J. (1984). *Blacks in college: A comparative study of students' success in Black and in White institutions*. San Francisco, CA: Jossey-Bass.

Foster, L. (2001). The not-so-invisible professors: White faculty at the Black college. *Urban Education, 36*, 611–629.

Gasman, M. (2013). *The changing face of historically Black colleges and universities*. Philadelphia, PA: Center for Minority Serving Institutions, University of Pennsylvania.

Gasman, M., Lundy-Wagner, V., Ransom, T., & Bowman, N., III. (2010). *Unearthing promise and potential: Our nation's historically Black colleges and universities*. San Francisco, CA: Jossey-Bass.

Harmon, N. (2012). The role of minority-serving institutions in national college completion goals. *Institute for Higher Education Policy*. Retrieved from http://www.eric.ed .gov/ERICWebPortal/recordDetail?accno=ED528603

Hughes, K. L., Rodriguez, O., Edwards, L., & Belfield, C. (2012). *Broadening the benefits of dual enrollment: Reaching underachieving and underprepared students with career-focused programs*. New York, NY: Community College Research Center.

Humphreys, J., & Korb, R. (2005). *Economic impact of the nation's historically Black colleges and universities* (NCES 2007-178). Washington, DC: National Center for Education Statistics.

Jaggars, S. S., & Xu, D. (2010). *Online learning in the Virginia community college system*. New York, NY: Community College Research Center.

Lundy-Wagner, V. (2013a). Contributing beyond the baccalaureate: Graduate and professional degree programs at HBCUs. In R. T. Palmer, A. A. Hilton, & T. P. Fountaine

(Eds.), *Graduate education at historically Black colleges and universities* (pp. 25–40). Charlotte, NC: Information Age Publishing.

Lundy-Wagner, V. (2013b). Is it really a man's world? Black men in science, technology, engineering and mathematics at historically Black colleges and universities. *Journal of Negro Education, 8*(2), 157–168.

Lundy-Wagner, V., & Gasman, M. (2011). When gender issues are not just about women: Reconsidering male students at historically Black colleges and universities. *Teachers College Record, 113*(5), 934–968.

Lundy-Wagner, V., Vultaggio, J., & Gasman, M. (2013). Preparing underrepresented students of color for doctoral success: The role of undergraduate institutions. *International Journal of Doctoral Studies, 8*, 151–172.

National Center for Education Statistics. (2013). *Integrated postsecondary education data system*. Washington, DC: U.S. Department of Education, Institute of Education Sciences.

Palmer, R. T., Davis, R. J., & Gasman, M. (2011). A matter of diversity, equity and necessity: The tension between Maryland's higher education system and its historically Black institutions over the OCR agreement. *Journal of Negro Education, 80*(2), 121–133.

Palmer, R. T., & Maramba, D. C. (in press-a). A delineation of Asian American and Latino/a students' experiences with faculty at an historically Black college and university. *Journal of College Student Development*.

Palmer, R. T., & Maramba, D. C. (in press-b). Racial microaggressions among Asian American and Latino/a students at an HBCU. *Journal of College Student Development*.

Parker, T. L. (2012). *The role of minority-serving institutions in redefining and improving developmental education*. Atlanta, GA: Southern Education Foundation.

Perna, L. W. (2001). The contribution of historically Black colleges and universities to the preparation of African Americans for faculty careers. *Research in Higher Education, 42*(3), 267–294.

Perna, L., Lundy-Wagner, V., Drezner, N. D., Gasman, M., Yoon, S., Bose, E., & Gary, S. (2009). The contribution of HBCUs to the preparation of African American women for STEM careers: A case study. *Research in Higher Education, 50*, 1–23.

Provasnik, S., Shafer, L. L., & Snyder, T. D. (2004). *Historically Black colleges and universities, 1976 to 2001* (NCES 2004-062). Washington, DC: National Center for Education Statistics.

Solórzano, D. G. (1995). The doctorate production and baccalaureate origins of African Americans in the sciences and engineering. *The Journal of Negro Education, 64*(1), 15–32.

Trower, C. A., & Chait, R. P. (2002). Faculty diversity: Too little for too long. *Harvard Magazine, 104*(4), 33–38.

Turley, R. N. L. (2009). College proximity: Mapping access to opportunity. *Sociology of Education, 82*(2), 126–146.

Wilson, M. (2009). *Struggle and success: The experiences of urban high school seniors participating in a dual enrollment program* (Unpublished doctoral dissertation). University of Pennsylvania, Philadelphia.

Wolf-Wendel, L. E. (1998). Models of excellence: The baccalaureate origins of successful African-American, European-American and Hispanic Women. *The Journal of Higher Education, 69*(2), 144–172.

VALERIE C. LUNDY-WAGNER is a senior research associate at the Community College Research Center at Teachers College, Columbia University.

NEW DIRECTIONS FOR HIGHER EDUCATION • DOI: 10.1002/he

8

Final Thoughts

C. Rob Shorette II

Significant attention in the 20th century was dedicated to understanding the dynamics of diversity and inclusion at historically and exclusively White institutions. The focus on predominantly White institutions (PWIs) is understandable considering that HBCUs comprise such a small percentage of all higher education institutions and, by the 1970s, the majority (over 75%) of African-American students were enrolled in PWIs. Unfortunately, the same attention was not given to understanding the dynamics of diversity and inclusion at HBCUs, and, as a result, researchers have limited literature to draw upon in that regard. In response to the void in research addressing issues of diversity at HBCUs, this volume has captured some of the unique contexts in which HBCUs experience issues of diversity and inclusion.

In many ways, this volume is the first of its kind when it comes to the level of inclusion it demonstrates. From highlighting the unique needs of lesbian, gay, bisexual, and transgender (LGBT) students to giving voice to non-Black students of color at HBCUs to introducing innovative ways for increasing the prominence of HBCUs in higher education policy efforts, the collective efforts of our contributing authors have further complicated the already complex issue of diversity at HBCUs and have established new directions for HBCU research, practice, and policy. Many questions remain unanswered about diversity and inclusion at HBCUs. Does diversity at HBCUs have an effect on educational outcomes in the same ways that researchers have found for students at PWIs? Can diversity at HBCUs be leveraged to enhance student success? Is there such a thing as a "critical mass" of non-Black students at an HBCU? How will Supreme Court rulings on affirmative action policies influence diversity at HBCUs? Can the benefits of an HBCU education (e.g., racial identity development, orientation to social justice) for non-Black students be quantified or conceptualized? Can or should we measure campus climates at HBCUs in the same way as they are measured at PWIs?

NEW DIRECTIONS FOR HIGHER EDUCATION, no. 170, Summer 2015 © 2015 Wiley Periodicals, Inc.
Published online in Wiley Online Library (wileyonlinelibrary.com) • DOI: 10.1002/he.20135

The possibilities are limitless, and by no means do these questions represent a comprehensive list of potential lines of scholarly inquiry. Ultimately, it is our hope that the research found in this volume will inspire and empower others to delve more deeply into the range of issues surrounding diversity at HBCUs, chart new paths to discovery, equip practitioners with the data to successfully support their students, and establish a robust foundation of literature for future researchers to build upon.

C. ROB SHORETTE II recently earned a PhD in higher education from Michigan State University. Dr. Shorette is an educator and researcher focused on diversity and equity in higher education, a former HBCU presidential aide, and an HBCU alumnus.

NEW DIRECTIONS FOR HIGHER EDUCATION • DOI: 10.1002/he

Index